Learning for Innovation in the Global Knowledge Economy

A European and South-East Asian Perspective

by Dimitrios Konstadakopulos

Centre for European Studies,

University of the West of England, Bristol, UK

intellect™
Bristol, UK
Portland, OR, USA

First published in UK in 2004 by
Intellect Books, PO Box 862, Bristol BS99 1DE, UK

First published in USA in 2004 by
Intellect Books, ISBS, 920 NE 58th Ave. Suite 300, Portland, Oregon 97213-3786, USA

Copy Editor: Holly Spradling
Cover Design: Gabriel Solomons

A catalogue record of this book is available from the British Library.
ISBN 1-84150-085-2

Printed in Great Britain by Antony Rowe Ltd.

ACKNOWLEDGEMENT

This study draws from projects supported by the Higher Education Regional Development Fund (Department for Education and Employment of the United Kingdom) (1998), the European Union's European Studies Programme (1999) and the Committee of South-East Asia Studies of the British Academy (2001). Each of these sources of financial support is gratefully acknowledged.

The author of this book is also grateful to the managers of regional companies in the West of England, Singapore and Johor, officials of local and regional institutions, and others, including an anonymous referee, who have given their time and expertise to provide information for this study and comment on the findings.

To the memory of my mother, Spyridoula

Contents

List of Tables   vii
List of Figures   xi
List of Abbreviations   xiii

Introduction   1
The origins of the research   1
The main research questions   3
The structure of the book   4

Part I:
The Embeddedness of Innovation in Regional Agglomerations   7

Chapter 1:
Fostering Innovation and Entrepreneurship   7
1.1 Innovative Environments and the Importance of Proximity   7
1.2 The Concept of the 'Innovative Milieu'   8
1.3 The Evolutionary Theory of Technological Change   11
1.4 The Importance of Agglomeration or Cluster Economies   13
1.5 Re-conceptualising the Role of Learning in Regional Development   15
1.6 The Exploitation of Collective Learning: An Easy and Inexpensive
Way to Innovate   17
1.7 The Importance of Networking for SMEs   18

Chapter 2:
Technological Innovation Policies in the EU and ASEAN Economies   23
2.1 The Emerging Global Knowledge Economy   23
2.2 The Evolutionary Development of Technological Policy in Europe   25
2.2.1 Policy Patterns in European Regional Agglomerations   27
2.2.2 The Industrial District of the West of England   31
2.3 The Evolving Nature of Technological Policy in ASEAN   34
    2.3.1 Singapore: Building a Capacity for Learning   36
    2.3.2 Malaysia's Technological Development   38
    2.3.3 The State of Johor: the Southern Gateway to Malaysia   41
    2.3.4 The Singapore-Johor Cross-Border Agglomeration and the
Logic of Spillover   42
2.4 EU-ASEAN Technological Co-operation   46

Part II:
The Empirical Comparative Analysis   53

Chapter 3:
Innovation in the West of England   53
3.1 The Profile of Innovative Regional Firms   53
3.2 Regional Innovators and their Sources of Innovation   55
3.3 Regional Collaboration in Product and Process Development   58
3.4 Inter-firm Linkages, Networks and Collaboration   59
3.5 The Effect of Regional Specific Advantages on Firms' Development   62
3.6 The Collective Learning Experience and Regional Channels of
Knowledge Acquisition   63

Chapter 4:
Innovation in the Singapore-Johor Agglomeration   69
4.1 The Profile of Innovative Regional Firms   69
4.2 Regional Innovators and their Sources of Innovation   71
4.3 Regional Collaboration in Product and Process Development   73
4.4 Inter-firm Linkages, Networks and Collaboration   74
4.5 The Effect of Regional Specific Advantages on Firms' Development   80
4.6 The Collective Learning Experience and Regional Channels of
Knowledge Acquisition   63

Chapter 5:
A Comparative Analysis of Patterns of Learning Behaviour and
Co-operation in the West of England and Singapore-Johor   87
5.1 A Statistical Analysis of the West of England Sample Survey   88
5.2 A Statistical Analysis of the Singapore-Johor Sample Survey   91
5.3 Industrial Districts, Innovative Milieux, Growth Triangles or
Global Knowledge Economies?   95

Part III:
Policy Lessons and Implications   101

Chapter 6:
The Relevance of the Economic, Political and Social
Environments of Europe and South-East Asia   101
6.1 Market Cultures in the Economies of Europe and South-East Asia   102
6.1.1 Competing Models of Development   106
6.1.2 Implications for Policy   110
6.2 Recommendations: Facilitating the Development of
Knowledge-intensive Enterprises   113

Bibliography   117
Appendix   135
Index   139

List of Tables

Table 2.1
Johor: Approved Projects by Country of Origin (1993-1997)

Table 2.2
Salient Issues in Complementarities between Singapore and Johor

Table 3.1
Size and Location of Sampled Firms used in the 1998-99 Survey in the West of England

Table 3.2
Innovation Output of Firms in Manufacturing and Services (1993-1998) in Three Urban
Agglomerations in the West of England, and Average R&D Intensity in 1998

Table 3.3
Principal Input of Learning for the Most Important Innovations for Firms in the West
of England

Table 3.4
Relationships with Suppliers and Subcontractors

Table 3.5
Geographical Location of Firms' Collaborating Suppliers and Subcontractors

Table 3.6
Destination of Sales

Table 3.7
Contributions to the Innovation Process by Firms' Customers

Table 3.8
The Importance of Local/Regional Links in the West of England

Table 3.9
Informal Contacts with Managers or Professionals from Other Local/Regional
Companies

Table 3.10
Regional Specific Advantages for Firms' Development

Table 3.11
Help or Advice Firms Received from Local Agencies (Government-Sponsored or

Otherwise) over the Last Five Years, and Rating of the Usefulness of Such Help/Advice

Table 3.12
Help and Support in Provision and Quality of Local Services in the West of England

Table 3.13
Regional and Local Channels of Knowledge Acquisition of High-Technology SMEs in the West of England: New Firm Start-Ups and Local Entrepreneurship

Table 3.14
Owners'/Founders' Origins

Table 3.15
Origins of Firms' Latest Research/Engineering/Management Staff

Table 3.16
New Local Start-Ups by Former Employees and Existing Linkages

Table 4.1
Size and Location of Sampled Firms used in the 1999 Survey in Singapore-Johor

Table 4.2
Innovation Output of Firms in Manufacturing and Services (1994-1999) in the Singapore and Johor Bahru Area, and Average R&D Intensity in 1998

Table 4.3
Principal Input of Learning for the Most Important Innovations for Firms in the Singapore-Johor Bahru Area

Table 4.4
Relationships with Suppliers and Subcontractors

Table 4.5
Contributions to the Innovation Process by Firms' Suppliers or Subcontractors

Table 4.6
Geographical Location of Firms' Collaborating Suppliers or Subcontractors

Table 4.7
Destination of Sales

Table 4.8
Contributions to the Innovation Process by Firms' Customers

Table 4.9
Geographical Location of Firms' Collaborating Customers

Table 4.10
Contribution of Collaborating Customers

Table 4.11
The Importance of Local/Regional Links in Singapore-Johor

Table 4.12
Informal Contacts with Managers or Professionals from Other Local/Regional Companies

Table 4.13
Regional Specific Advantages for Firms' Development

Table 4.14
Help or Advice Firms Received from Local Agencies (Government-Sponsored or Otherwise) over the Last Five Years, and Rating of the Usefulness of such Help/Advice

Table 4.15
Help and Support in Provision and Quality of Local Services in Singapore-Johor Area

Table 4.16
Regional and Local Channels of Knowledge Acquisition of High-Technology SMEs in the Singapore-Johor Area: New Firm Start-Ups and Local Entrepreneurship

Table 4.17
Owners'/Founders' Origins

Table 4.18
Owners'/Founders' Experience and Qualifications

Table 4.19
Origins of Firms' Latest Research/Engineering/Management Staff

Table 4.20
New Local Start-Ups by Former Employees and Existing Linkages

Table 5.1
The Principal Factors of the West of England Data Survey

Table 5.2
Regression Analyses

Table 5.3
The Principal Factors of the Singapore-Johor Data Survey

Table 5.4
Regression Analyses

Table 5.5
Main Characteristics of Small Innovative and Knowledge-intensive Firms in the West of England and Singapore-Johor Agglomerations

List of Figures

Figure 1.1
Science Systems plc: External Sources of Innovative Ideas

Figure 2.1
Intra-ASEAN Exports

Figure 3.1
Clustering of Innovative SMEs in the West of England

Figure 3.2
Sources of Learning in the West of England

Figure 3.3
Collaboration in Product/Process Development in the West of England

Figure 4.1
Clustering of High-Technology SMEs in Singapore-Johor Bahru

Figure 4.2
Sources of Learning in Singapore-Johor

Figure 4.3
Collaboration in Product/Process Development in Singapore-Johor

Figure 5.1
Cluster Analysis of the West of England Data Survey

Figure 5.2
Cluster Analysis of the Singapore-Johor Data Survey

List of Abbreviations

AFTA
Asian Free Trade Association
APEC
Asia Pacific Economic Co-operation
ASEAN
Association of Southeast Asian Nations
CoR
Committee of the Regions
DTI
Department of Trade and Industry
EDB
Economic Development Board
EMU
[European] Economic and Monetary Union
ERDF
European Regional Development Fund
EU
European Union
FDI
Foreign direct investment
GDP
Gross domestic product
GNP
Gross national product
GREMI
Groupement Européen des Milieux Innovateurs
MIDA
Malaysian Industrial Development Authority
OECD
Organisation for Economic Co-operation and Development
PAP
Political Action Party in Singapore
R&D
Research and development
SIJORI
Singapore-Johor-Riau (Growth Triangle)
SMEs
Small and medium-sized enterprises
TNCs
Trans-National Corporations
UMNO

United Malays National Organisation
WTO
World Trade Organization

Introduction

The origins of the research

A large part of industry in the developed and developing countries consists of indigenous small and medium-sized enterprises (SMEs). Within countries, the spread of such SMEs is variable. Some regions, such as the South West of England, have a relatively large number of indigenous SMEs[1] and a strong culture of entrepreneurship[2], and this is often reflected in high levels of self-employment. Previous research in the South West of England and South Wales[3] has indicated that almost a half of all regional SMEs lack the resources to benefit from the adoption of new technologies. Such innovation-averse SMEs are also resistant to change, and lack an overall innovation strategy. However, the research also identified small, dynamic local companies with a high research and development (R&D) intensity and high innovative output in terms of radical product innovation. The success of some industrial districts in Europe and America (for example, Third Italy, Baden-Württemberg, Sophia-Antipolis, Oxford, Cambridge and Silicon Valley), and the emergence of new ones in East and South-East Asia (for example, the Singapore-Johor-Riau growth triangle) indicates a new model of development based on the concept of knowledge-based economy and the process of *learning for innovation*, particularly at the local/regional level. However, very little is known about learning for innovation at regional levels.

Learning has become one of the most popular concepts in regional development because of the relationship between agglomeration economies, knowledge and innovation. It is also often asserted that the learning process for innovation and economic growth is closely associated with the regional dynamics of integration, as well as with the process of globalisation. However, the globalisation process itself, coupled with the most recent economic crisis in Asia, has a complex effect on the dynamics of change within Europe and the ASEAN region (Association of Southeast Asian Nations), as well as on other regional groupings. Moreover, the single European market and Economic and Monetary Union (EMU) have implications for economic and industrial co-operation between the European Union (EU) and the ASEAN region. It is important, therefore, not only to understand how learning for innovation - a necessary determinant for economic growth - is taking place in the European and ASEAN regions, but also to investigate new ways of strengthening the linkages between the private sectors of the ASEAN region and the EU through the improvement of existing arrangements or the establishment of new collaborative ones. In this respect, innovation and the promotion of SMEs[4] have justifiably become priority areas of co-operation in EU-ASEAN relations.

Both globalisation and regional integration are affecting regional growth and dynamic change, through the activities of smaller firms and clusters of SMEs. Regional integration implies that most sub-regions and urban areas around the world remain much more intimately linked with their particular hinterland. This is particularly so in

Europe, and to some extent in the ASEAN region, where one can observe the accelerating integration of adjacent countries and of their respective economic actors (including SMEs) (Breslin and Higgott, 2000). In this respect, Europe is a prime example of how areas and localities function within an innovative milieu influenced by rapid globalisation and European integration. These reflections lead to some interesting empirical questions, which were investigated during fieldwork visits to the West of England, as well as to Singapore and the southern part of the Malaysian State of Johor.[5] During the last fifteen years, the economic growth of some regional agglomerations in Europe and South-East Asia has received attention from a number of researchers and decision-makers. In this book, the West of England M4/M5 corridors (i.e. the areas surrounding the two motorways passing through the region, from London to South Wales, and from Birmingham to Exeter) and the Singapore-Johor agglomeration (part of the Singapore-Johor-Riau growth triangle) have been chosen as the appropriate areas of research. A number of factors are considered in the context of innovation and learning in the manufacturing and services sectors. Foreign direct investment, the operation of trans-national corporations (TNCs), and regional or national technology policies are also to be examined, as they are important determinants in the integration process of the above agglomerations.

SMEs in general play an important role in the economic development of both the EU and the ASEAN region. In Singapore, there are about 89,000 SMEs, representing 90% of the total number of companies in the economy[6]. The remaining 7,000 are either foreign or large companies. SMEs in Singapore employ nearly half of the working population and contribute to approximately one third of the total value added, while in Malaysia their contribution is probably much higher.

Rapidly developing and knowledge-intensive SMEs (the focus of this investigation) can be found in a wide range of sectors in the ASEAN economies, as well as in Europe. It was envisaged that by selecting two samples of high-technology SMEs displaying high growth from both agglomerations, this would be a representative sample of the diversified high-technology sectors as well as a good example of the vitality of European and ASEAN SMEs. These firms may not only be conscious of productivity and quality but also have existing partners for technological collaboration in the European or ASEAN marketplace. They may also have linkages with similar high-technology SMEs in other parts of the world. It is postulated that in the global economy SMEs need to search far afield for partnerships, markets and technological know-how. Therefore, the scope for beneficial technology partnering and learning for innovation between companies from the EU and the ASEAN region is enormous. As trade and investment between the two regions have been developing (for instance, the EU is second only to the US in non-oil exports from Singapore (EIU, 1998)), a wide range of economic co-operative activities in promoting mutual understanding among SMEs' managers are taking place. These activities also include linkages with high-tech sectors and collaboration in science and technology. For example, the EU, in its 1996 policy document entitled 'Creating new dynamics in EU-ASEAN relations', encourages the development of closer links between SMEs. In the following year, the ASEAN-EU Partenariat '97 in Singapore - involving seven ASEAN host countries, as well as the members of the European Union - highlighted the importance of the ever-strengthening relationship between EU and ASEAN SMEs. In 2001, and in the context of certain wariness in some European countries about engaging in the region, the European Commission published its Communication entitled 'Europe and Asia: A Strategic Framework for Enhanced Partnerships'.[7] In relation to ASEAN, the Commission expressed the wish to enhance co-operation between the two regions, particularly in new-technology sectors.

The main research questions

The objective of this book is to develop a knowledge base on the learning and innovative behaviour of clustered SMEs in the South West of England and the Singapore-Johor cross-border area. Specifically, the factors which stimulate or inhibit innovation (inter-firm, regional/local, institutional or structural) are identified. Advancing the understanding of learning behaviour patterns of SMEs is crucial to improving the competitiveness of regional agglomerations around the world.

The book will contribute in particular to:

* the production of new empirical data on the evolving structure and composition of local and/or regional SMEs
* the improvement of SMEs' innovative performance, growth and competitiveness
* the support of the collaborative learning process, and promotion of a culture of innovation and institutional adaptation and change
* the enhancement of the relationship between SMEs and key support institutions
* the identification of new patterns of training, learning and assessment of SMEs' managers and workforce
* the relevance of the emerging knowledge-based economy

The focus of the book will be on the role of collective and collaborative learning processes that are taking place in the two dynamic regional clusters of innovative technology-intensive SMEs under investigation. These two clusters - the sub-regional agglomeration of the West of England M4/M5 corridors, and the Singapore-Johor cross-border area - are manageable in terms of size and logistics, offer willing collaborators, and are credible as examples of innovative activity. They provided the sampling frame for an interview survey of more than 90 randomly selected technology-intensive SMEs - 61 in the West of England and 30 from the Singapore-Johor area. Subsequently, a database was built, mainly as binary (yes/no) or discrete (qualitative judgement) variables. The sample was chosen to reflect the balance between manufacturing and services within the firms in each cluster. The following research questions were investigated through a number of work packages:

Do we observe an innovative milieu in which collective and collaborative learning exists in the two high-technology clusters of the West of England and Singapore-Johor?

Can we identify a different learning behaviour in local firms with respect to different innovative activities and different size of firm?

Do we observe that small firms take advantage of the agglomeration's collective learning?

Do we expect breakthrough innovations to be positively correlated with collective learning?

Several approaches are explored, using factor, cluster and regression analyses. The methodology of these types of statistical analysis has been described in detail in Rabellotti (1997) and Capello (1999); therefore, the emphasis in the following chapters is on the results of the analyses, rather than the methodological and theoretical approaches involved.

Firstly, an attempt is made to conceptualise the processes of learning and knowledge transfer over time and in their spatial context. Special attention is given to the cluster model of development and the extensive literature in which it appears. Secondly, the book investigates, at an empirical level, learning processes involved in the recent growth of high-technology SMEs in the West of England and the Singapore-Johor cross-border area. Drawing upon a variety of qualitative and quantitative research methods and sampling techniques, it analyses locally based SMEs in order to assess how learning for innovation is shaped by specific factors. Although the two clusters differ in scale and composition, they are similar in that they historically focus on engineering and business services, and have a global reputation for research and scientific activity.

The empirical results identify some important behavioural patterns of regionally based SMEs in relation to learning for innovation. The conclusion drawn is that learning and the acquisition of knowledge is an important determinant of innovative activities in high-technology milieux, and could provide the basis for technological policy on SMEs in Europe and ASEAN.

The structure of the book

This book is divided into three parts. Part I sets out the theoretical framework for the empirical analysis. Here we consider questions about the significance of the spatial dimension in conducting research, and about the innovative activities of SMEs. In addition, the views that have come to dominate the debate on innovation in the emerging global knowledge-based economy are discussed.

Part I contains the following two chapters:

(a) Chapter 1 examines the theoretical concept of innovative milieux that has been developed in Europe. It seeks to contribute to the debate by evaluating the extent to which the institutional context and local setting are important determinants in influencing the learning behaviour and innovative capacity of high-technology SMEs.

(b) Chapter 2 considers the evolutionary development of technological policies in Europe and ASEAN in the context of the broader debate on the emerging knowledge-based economy. At the same time, it discusses in more detail the extent to which such technological policies have influenced the development of two regional agglomerations: the West of England and the Singapore-Johor cross-border area. Finally, we examine the scope and development of EU-ASEAN technological co-operation in the light of renewed efforts by the two regional groupings.

Part II turns to the comparative empirical analysis of the two regional agglomerations:

(a) Chapter 3 comprises the European case study: the West of England. This study shows how regional SMEs link, network and collaborate with each other with regard to innovation. It also attempts to identify the collective learning experiences of such firms and to highlight how institutional and local setting affects their development.

(b) Chapter 4 presents the results from the empirical investigation in the Singapore-Johor cross-border area in a similar manner.

(c) Chapter 5 presents the comparative analysis of patterns of learning behaviour and co-operation within surveyed SMEs in the West of England and the Singapore-Johor area. In seeking to understand the principal factors that underpin innovative behaviour, and in order to band together firms that share the same characteristics, factor and cluster analyses are employed. Both types of analysis help us to identify the 'ideal' type of company postulated in the theoretical concept of innovative milieux examined in Part I.

Finally, in Part III we look at the wider economic, political and social environment of Europe and South-East Asia, and the way they construct their own distinctive market cultures. We also discuss the European and ASEAN models of development and their implications for policy. The book concludes with some recommendations on how to facilitate the development of regional SMEs' innovative activities in the global knowledge-based economy.

Notes

[1] The South West of England has 30,746 businesses per million of population, whereas the UK as a whole has 26,837 (Enterprise and Prism Research, Final Report, 2000)

[2] *Sunday Times*, 'Southwest is the top spot for entrepreneurs', 7 April 2002. This article, drawing from a study conducted by Barclays Bank, reports that, with the exception of London, the cities and towns of the South West of England have the highest business start-ups in the UK as a percentage of population.

[3] The research was based on field studies and a company survey of over 200 SMEs and was carried out by the author in the South West of England and South Wales (January 1996 - February 1997).

[4] There are different definitions of SMEs in the three countries in this study. Malaysia prefers the term 'Small and Medium Scale Industries' (SMIs), which are defined as entities with annual sales turnover not exceeding RM 25 million and having not more than 150 full-time employees. In Singapore, SMEs are classified according to the amount of local equity, business activities, number of employees and fixed assets at net book value (see the *APEC Survey on Small and Medium Enterprises*, 1994, Singapore: APEC Secretariat). For the purpose of this study, the European definition of SMEs is used, which includes all companies with less than 250 employees.

[5] These fieldwork visits were made in the context of two identical and consecutive research projects: (a) *Facilitating the Learning Behaviour of Small Innovative Firms*, supported by the Higher Education Regional Development Fund, (Department for Education and Employment of the United Kingdom), October 1998- September 1999; (b) *Reinforcing the Learning Behaviour of Small Innovative Firms of the ASEAN Region: A New Approach to Regional Integration*, supported by the EU's European Studies Programme, February 1999-August 1999.

[6] Singapore Department of Statistics, 2000.

[7] COM(2001) 469 final.

Part I: The Embeddedness of Innovation in Regional Agglomerations

Chapter 1:

Fostering Innovation and Entrepreneurship

1.1 Innovative Environments and the Importance of Proximity

Most firms in Europe and South-East Asia are well aware of the importance of innovation in achieving commercial success. However, relatively few firms are becoming innovators; most are content to adopt existing innovations. It seems that it is not only difficult to define precisely what innovation is, but also difficult to measure it, as it is not always directly reflected in the profitability of firms. It is more or less accepted that innovation means the creation of a better product or process. Dyson Ltd., based in the West of England, did exactly that when James Dyson and his research team designed a new type of high quality vacuum cleaner. This innovative product has been an outstanding commercial success, with sales of over £3 billion worldwide.

The problem of precisely defining innovation is compounded by the erroneous belief that the development of new products or processes adds to firms' costs and increases risks. On the contrary, it has been found that innovation brings far higher returns than ordinary business activities (Klomp and Leeuwen, 2001, p. 359)[1]. The suggestion that innovation-averse firms need to challenge their assumptions and start encouraging creativity and experimentation is supported by the findings of the present study. In addition, and most importantly, these firms must draw from the human capital of their region and learn from the best practice of their regional breakthrough innovators.

Of course, the nature of innovative activities varies markedly across trading blocks, as well as across areas belonging to the same block, owing to the different profiles of the areas' human capital in relation to education, age, occupation, wealth, and infrastructure endowment. For these reasons, within Europe and ASEAN some areas have more innovative companies than others. The South West of England[2], and in particular its north-eastern part - the West of England - has a large number of indigenous firms operating at the leading edge of technology, especially in advanced engineering, aerospace, telecommunications and electronics. Well-known indigenous world-class companies such as BAe (formerly British Aerospace), GNK-Westland, Messier-Dowty, Rolls Royce, Racal-Thorn, Rotork, Renishaw, and Smiths Industries, as well as many others, play a vital role in creating a dynamic regional economy. Alongside them, a number of multinational companies such as Hewlett Packard, Honda, Intel, Motorola, Lucent Technologies, and STMicroelectronics have moved in to exploit the region's knowledge and skilled workforce, its business atmosphere and reputation for innovation.

The Singapore-Johor cross-border area has a rather smaller number of indigenous high-technology companies and a large number of multinational companies operating in electronics, telecommunications, engineering and chemicals. Some of the indigenous companies, such as Aztech, Creative Technology and SingTel, have become world players in multimedia applications and telecommunications. It is nevertheless the presence of multinationals from Japan, the US and Europe, such as Compaq, Hewlett Packard, IBM, Matsushita, Motorola, NEC, Philips, Sony, Seagate, Siemens and STMicroelectronics to name a few, that has led to technological innovation in the area.

However, it is important to pay attention as much to the innovation processes, external sources of innovative ideas, and extent of innovative inter-firm linkages, as to the factors affecting the efficiency of regional or local economies. In addition, the institutionally embedded nature of the innovation process makes strong claims about the role of the regional/local context as a fundamental factor. In the following chapters we examine how far these propositions can be applied in practice to the West of England agglomeration and the Singapore-Johor cross-border area.

1.2 The Concept of the 'Innovative Milieu'

In order to understand the importance of regional innovation in the West of England and the Singapore-Johor cross-border area, it will be necessary to present the latest theoretical concepts found in economic and management disciplines. It should be pointed out that no major new theories on innovation and entrepreneurship have been developed since those of early economists such as Adam Smith, David Ricardo, Alfred Marshall and Joseph Schumpeter. Perhaps Galar's reminder of the ancient dictum *natura horret vacuum* - that there are no empty places waiting for new theories to be nested (2000, p. 288) - is appropriate in this context. However, during the last fifteen years, two concepts complementing the theories have emerged.[3] These concentrate respectively on the *innovative milieu* (innovative environment), and on *technological change*.

In the late 1980s and early 1990s, a number of European economists[4], mainly from Italy, Switzerland, France and the UK, and known as the GREMI group (*Groupement Européen des Milieux Innovateurs*), elaborated on the theories of innovation and entrepreneurship and introduced the concept of the *innovative milieu* (*milieu innovateur*). The central theoretical assumption of the milieu approach is that the *innovative milieu* - that is, the socio-economic environment of a region - is produced by the interactions of firms, institutions and labour. The GREMI group introduced the concept of the *collective learning* process[5], which increases the creativity and continuous innovation of firms belonging to that milieu (Camagni, 1991; 1995), although the concept has only recently been fully developed (Rabellotti, 1997; Bramanti and Ratti, 1997; Keeble *et al*, 1997 and 1999; Camagni and Rabellotti, 1997; Capello, 1999; Lawson and Lorenz, 1999; Helmsing, 2001). In the milieu, the process of learning is brought about by the activity of participating actors, the mobility of labour, and the interconnections between suppliers, customers and subcontractors. It is greatly assisted by face-to-face contacts between actors, and these are facilitated by geographical proximity.

Some fifty years ago, Alfred Marshall commented on the importance of such proximity for the steel industry in the 'industrial district' of Sheffield. However, the GREMI group points to different stages of development and different typologies of districts. They suggest that the evolution from clustering through to industrial districts and then towards milieux requires particular pre-conditions (Capello, 1999). The process of collective learning in an innovative milieu is attributed to the mobility of the local labour market, with the market supplying its own knowledge. Local cumulative knowledge may be grasped by local actors (particularly SMEs) and is the source of a dynamic comparative advantage. If these pre-conditions do not exist, what we have is simply a traditional, static Marshallian industrial district (Camagni and Rabellotti, 1997, p. 139). As Capello points out, when the local actors grasp collective learning and turn it into profits, then, and only then, does an innovative milieu emerge. The profits will partly remunerate the risks for innovation and uncertainty (Capello, 1999, p. 357).

The GREMI group attempts to explain the reasons why firms try to exploit this collective learning. This may depend on the willingness and capacity of local SMEs to absorb it, as well as on the awareness that such learning exists. In addition, the exploitation of collective learning is inversely related to the size of the firm (Capello, 1999, pp. 357-358).

In this respect, the collective learning process is seen to generate radical rather than incremental innovation. The firm's ability to produce a radical or breakthrough innovation is based on new knowledge, and scientific and managerial expertise, which stems from the historical process of cumulative know-how and learning processes (Rabellotti, 1997, p. 165; Gregersen and Johnson, 1997, p. 486). Once a firm needs to achieve a radical product innovation, it is more likely to exploit the existence of a large pool of skilled local labour, which brings with it accumulated knowledge. Process innovation requires incremental changes, and is the outcome of internal knowledge within each firm (Konstadakopulos, 1997). The same analogy applies to the size of the firm for the exploitation of collective learning (Rabellotti, 1997; Capello, 1999). A large and rather secretive firm is likely to exploit its internal resources, and most unlikely to participate in the socialisation process of creative knowledge. A small firm is more likely to tap into the region's collective learning and adapt it to its potentially different needs once the externality is present. According to recent findings in the Italian high-tech milieux, such firms are likely to be found in a high-technology milieu, characterised by the creation of new firms in which research ideas and technological innovations are shared and diffused (Capello, 1999; Bellandi, 2002). This process reduces the uncertainty inherent in technological innovation, and may allow the smaller firms to survive.

However, the capacity of local firms to exploit collective learning materialises when they can turn knowledge into a business idea (Capello, 1999, p. 357). Thus, either an emerging group of local entrepreneurs may willingly share this knowledge among themselves, or a local/regional institution could codify and diffuse such knowledge (Teubal, 1997, p. 1170; Helmsing, 2001, p. 303).

Geographical proximity also helps the establishment of horizontal linkages and activities between economic actors (particularly between SMEs) across sectors and technologies (Kirat and Lung, 1999, p. 30). However, it is also appropriate to mention here that the collective learning process involves not only technology but many other externalities derived from experience in joint marketing, project generation, management and organisation (Teubal, 1997, pp. 1183-4). Kamann effectively describes the intra-actor organisation and behaviour pattern at the milieu level:

> The more activities actors transfer to other actors, the more activity chains of actors are interwoven and become interdependent; the more relationships are embedded into a distinctly homogeneous cognitive set of the network, the more synergy accrues, the more the network is entitled to bear the name 'innovative'. The more the territorial is prominent - both in the production links, the selection environment and cognitive embeddedness - the more pronounced the role of the particular milieux will be.
>
> (Kamann, 1997, pp. 376-377)

The socialisation of managers of SMEs is quite important here. This socialisation is known as the *cafeteria effect*, and is an important element in building a local entrepreneurial capacity. Interpersonal linkages through professional associations, clubs, families and other social organisations are vital channels for sharing and diffusing research ideas, technological innovations and expertise within the region.

The examples of Italian innovative milieux indicate that, after the establishment of the milieu, 'a positive feedback effect arises which reinforces the elements of continuity (stable labour market, stable inter-SMEs' linkages) and of dynamic synergies (interactive mechanisms leading to innovation)' (Capello, 1999). Stable labour relations mean that, although there is an apparent labour mobility within the milieu, there is hardly any inflow or outflow of skilled workforce that may destabilise it.

As noted earlier, the innovative milieu approach has incorporated and improved the Marshallian concept of the *industrial district*, but also parallels other recent theorisation and research traditions within the framework of the endogenous growth approach, such as local production systems and Post-Fordist flexible production specialisation[6]. Moreover, the milieu approach puts forward two more elements that distinguish it from the above approaches: the collective learning process that enhances local creativity, and the reduction of the elements of uncertainty that are inherent in technological development and the innovative process (Camagni, 1991, p. 3).

So far, the GREMI group has not been able to define exactly what are the overall necessary conditions that make up an innovative milieu. For some time now, questions have been raised on how innovative milieux come into being (i.e. whether through luck or historical accident) and whether they represent a general model of regional development or a specialised model suited to highly unique circumstances (Bergman, 1991, p. 284). The above uncertainty has apparently led some of the GREMI researchers to attempt to distinguish between the endogenous, exogenous and techno-metropolitan milieu. They argue that the endogenous milieu arises around territorial networks of SMEs whose 'economic relations are rooted in history', under favourable cultural conditions. The exogenous innovative milieu arises from the establishment of subsidiaries of large companies in the area, while the third type of milieu arises from the proximity of metropolitan agglomerations and urbanisation effects (Kamann, 1997, pp. 380-381). One criticism of the innovative milieu concept is that it has only been used in high-technology areas, implying erroneously that innovativeness and high technology are the same thing (Lawson, 1997, pp. 11-12). Sternberg in particular has argued that the innovative milieu approach lacks operational feasibility, but the evidence to support this has been limited (Sternberg, 1996a, pp. 533-4). Storper argues that the GREMI group has never been able to specify the potential mechanism and process by which such milieux function, nor the economic rationalism by which milieux foster innovation. A tautology is apparent in that 'there is a circularity: innovation occurs because of a milieu, and a milieu is what exists in regions where there is innovation' (Storper, 1995, p. 203).

An examination of the literature also reveals that so far there are very few cases of regional agglomerations explained by the innovative milieu approach (Sternberg, 1996a, p. 533). However, it is important to point out that innovative milieux grow very slowly. Moreover, existing case studies undertaken by the GREMI group focus mainly on regions or agglomerations that are situated in the centre of Europe (Paci and Usai, 2000), and that are innovative and performing well. But the group has little to say about non-innovative milieux and what distinguishes them from innovative milieux, although more recently Capello has highlighted the importance of local pre-conditions that facilitate the exploitation of collective learning (Capello, 1999). Further criticisms concern the precise contribution that networks will eventually make to our understanding of regions (Bergman, 1991, p. 286), and the inadequate integration of the theory of networks into the region-oriented innovative milieu approach (Sternberg, 1996a, p. 532). The reason for such poor integration is that the innovative milieu approach is biased too heavily towards small firms and the incubator role of the milieu for innovation to be supported; it neglects some aspects of reality.

Notwithstanding the above criticisms, the GREMI group economists contribute substantially to our understanding of the process of regional development. They argue that the economic process is fundamentally about the creation of knowledge and resources. Both derive from the process of creativity of economic actors who are - at least in part - dependent on their milieu (Storper, 1995, pp. 203-204). Undoubtedly the innovative milieu approach has policy implications, given its capacity to enable decisions-makers to adopt measures that could create, duplicate or stimulate innovative milieux. Finally, the GREMI group links the concept of both the innovative milieu and the innovative network with the evolutionary theory of technological change proposed by Nelson, Winter, Freeman and Dosi, which acknowledges fully the importance of the learning process (Camagni, 1991, pp. 10-11; Capello, 1999).

1.3 The Evolutionary Theory of Technological Change

The evolutionary economics pioneered in the mid-1980s by Nelson and Winter, and developed and presented by Dosi and others (Nelson and Winter, 1982; Dosi *et al*,

1988), has identified aspects of regional economy that underlie innovative agglomerations of both the high- and low-technology variety. The evolutionary school claims that technological change is dependent on a path or trajectory. Interdependent choices are made by actors about changes made over time, which are entirely different from those of orthodox economics. These choices, however, have a spatial dimension, in other words a degree of territorialisation. The evolutionary economists emphasise that successful economies are not now based on the Fordist regime of mass production methods, but instead are orientated toward technological learning and the absolute advantage it is generating for learners (Storper, 1995, pp. 207-8). As Johanson et al. note, the evolution theory is intimately related to knowledge and learning (2001, p. 411). The evolutionary theorists have put forward the *learning-by-doing* and *learning-by-using* processes, which promote creativity and bring about successive incremental innovations. Firms studied in the evolutionary approach innovate to a lesser degree than those analysed in the study of innovative milieux. The innovation that they do achieve is the result of improving the quality of their products and purchasing advanced equipment and machinery. Peyrache-Dadeau considers an additional process, that of *learning-by-interacting*, in which 'firms adjust their specialised know-how through relations among themselves' (Peyrache-Dadeau, 1997, p. 314).

Thus the evolutionary theory perceives innovation as an endogenous process, taking the form of continuous incremental improvements within *path-dependent* trajectories based on existing problem-solving methods and practices (Gordon, 1991, p. 186). Sengenberger and Pyke have argued that there are two possible paths which firms, industries or regions have to take in order to meet the challenges of international competition. One is the so-called *low road* 'through low labour cost and a deregulated labour market', and the other is the *high road* 'of constructive competition, based on efficiency enhancement and innovation' (Sengenberger and Pyke, 1992, pp. 11-13). In this context, technological change is seen as occurring in the form of localised trajectories, which are based on common views about problems and solutions. Such trajectories are based at the intersection of networks belonging to different planes. These planes are in economic space, geographical space, and socio-cultural space (Kamann, 1991, p. 36). However, all production systems are faced with uncertainty and the imperfect information intrinsic in technological development and innovative processes. The way that such uncertainty is resolved is through *conventions* of a production network and its agglomeration. However, the example of leading innovative small- and medium-sized high-technology firms in Silicon Valley and elsewhere reveals that these enterprises move beyond the narrowly incrementalist forms of innovation envisaged by evolutionary theory (Gordon, 1991, p. 187). Despite this criticism, the contribution of the evolutionary school of technological change parallels that of the innovative milieu in emphasising the importance of learning as a major feature of economic development.

It is important to add here that small and large firms play different roles in innovation activity. The literature on small firm innovation draws mainly on Joseph Schumpeter's interpretation of the entrepreneur in the process of 'creative destruction', in which innovation and the size of firm are positively correlated. Major innovations have been traditionally associated with large multinationals. However, the empirical evidence of the role of SMEs in the innovation process is inconclusive. Small firms are generally regarded as making the most significant contribution to radical innovations in high-technology fields such as computers and biotechnology, while large firms make a significant contribution to innovation in medium technology (Parker, 2001, pp. 379-380). A recent empirical study of innovative behaviour in SMEs in the car industry in Italy suggests that there is a trade-off between a firm's internal capabilities and external sources of information. However, technologically competent firms tend to structure innovation internally by creating an R&D department and investing heavily in information technology (Calabrese, 2002). A study on the innovation of small firms in Cyprus - a small developing country - also suggests that strategic expenditure in R&D by the firm, as well as co-operation with external technology providers and other information sources, is conducive to innovation (Hadjimanolis, 2000). Furthermore, it appears that the innovative capabilities of small firms are conditioned by the national and regional environments in which they are embedded (Cooke et al., 2000, pp. 36-37).

1.4 The Importance of Agglomeration or Cluster Economies

Generally speaking, geographical proximity or regional clustering of SMEs brings few benefits, although it is a necessary pre-condition for their development. Clustering is the tendency of companies in similar lines of business to concentrate geographically. California's Silicon Valley - the industrial strip between San Francisco and San Jose in northern California - is the most well-known recent example of agglomeration. There are quite a few clusters in Europe that resemble Silicon Valley, from the high-tech agglomeration of Cambridge's *Silicon Fen* to low-tech ones, such as northern Italy's textile and ceramic tile businesses.

An attempt to construct an evolutionary scheme of economic development based on these ideas was made by Porter (1990; 1996) and by Kanter (1995). The most competitive industries, they argue, tend to be highly integrated (*clustered*), with favourable consequences for learning, innovation and competitive advantage. Feser makes a distinction between two core dimensions of clusters: economic and geographical clustering. Some end-market sectors such as consumer electronics may be both economically and geographically clustered, while in other sectors, such as basic consumer services, clustering is irrelevant (Feser, 1998, p. 25). According to Porter, the regionally concentrated cluster, and not the individual industry, is the appropriate unit of analysis on empirical grounds. The reason is that externalities, including collective learning, 'may be powerful among related industries' (Porter, 1996, p. 85).

The existence of regional clusters is a topic that has been well documented during the last two decades (Pinch and Henry, 1999; Hendry et al., 2000; Beaudry, 2001; Cooke, 2002). The four terms that we have already employed for denoting clusters - agglomerations, growth triangles, industrial districts and innovative milieux - have been supplemented by terms such as *technological districts*, *local production systems*, *systems areas*, *small firm territorial systems* and *metropolitan areas*. They have been familiar features for some time, especially for understanding regional development. It was primarily the influential work of Porter, *The Competitive Advantage of Nations*, that revived the cluster debate and highlighted the importance of agglomeration economies in relation to local/regional development and the importance of clustered SMEs. Both Steiner and Lagendijk, in their expositions on the attractiveness of clusters, discuss the changing character of regional specialisation and cluster policies (Steiner, 1998; Lagendijk, 1998). Porter indicates that regional clusters are often a mixture of mature and emerging industries, as opposed to those which are exclusively high technology, knowledge-intensive, innovative and newly established (Porter, 1996, pp. 87-88). More recently, Porter argues that location becomes more, not less, important in the context of the global economy. 'The enduring competitive advantages ... lie increasingly in local things, important in a global economy' (quoted in the *Financial Times*, 12 November 1998).

Familiarity with clusters is important in understanding regional technological policy (Diez, 2001, pp. 909-910). The main reason for this is that cluster policies appear to be justified for the development of an area, especially when faced with the threat of globalisation. Clusters, being very flexible albeit 'chaotic' concepts[7], could be seen by decision-makers as policy orientated, either to large technology sectoral policies, which cover a substantial part of the regional economy, or to the creation of networks of small SMEs (see DTI, 1998). In the 1990s some supranational organisations, such as the OECD and the EU, influenced by Porter's contribution, engaged in the debate on the adoption of policies based on agglomeration or clustering. In Europe, regional policies in several regions are geared to clustering. Cluster policies at regional level have been adopted by some of the German *Länder* (i.e. Nordrhein-Westphalen and Baden-Württemberg), some of the autonomous communities in Spain (i.e. Catalonia and the Basque Country), and by Northern Ireland (Lagendijk, 1998, p. 319). Lagendijk shows that cluster policies and initiatives in the UK emerged out of sectoral policies that were evolved from the *industrial district* model and have developed in the context of a more comprehensive policy in Scotland, Wales and Northern Ireland, rather than England (Lagendijk, 1998, pp. 328-330). However, more recently the English regions, including the South West, have started to adopt cluster policies, and this will be discussed in greater detail in the following chapter.

In South-East Asia, governments have repeatedly expressed a desire to foster high-tech clusters and corridors, like America's Silicon Valley. For instance, the government of Malaysia has attracted over 800 high-technology companies in its ambitious *Multimedia Super Corridor* south of Kuala Lumpur. The State of Johor in Malaysia is also promoting the concept of industrial clusters for selected strategic industries in high and low technology (Mohamed, 1998, pp. 157-158). Singapore is currently concentrating and investing in R&D in cutting-edge technologies in three clusters of national importance: electronics, chemicals and engineering.

A closer examination of the evolving regional policies in the South West of England and neighbouring Wales, as well as in other European regions, indicates a disposition of local/regional decision-makers towards collaboration rather than competition. For instance, the regional technology plan of Wales supports firm networking and collaboration, and the building of the region's social capital (*Financial Times*, 22 October

1998). Associational tendencies which connect both small and large firms around a supply chain (such as the *AIRLINE* association of the aerospace industry, the *West of England Aerospace Forum* in the South West of England, or the *Welsh Opto-electronics Forum*) have also been promoted as important initiatives for regional development, as such policy-making clusters serve political interests. The clusters provide an opportunity to sub-national entities (especially new regional governance) to target particular industries and develop an industrial policy, as well as perhaps filling the gap created by the free market that emanates from supranational entities for limiting or abolishing industrial policy. However, according to Porter, who has created a consultancy company for identifying and auditing clusters, a 'regional policy should promote specialisation, upgrading and trade among regions'. Cluster formation can be encouraged by locating specialised infrastructure and institutions in areas where factor endowments, past industrial activity, or even historical accidents have resulted in concentrations of economic activity (Porter, 1996, p. 88). The process of learning links well with the above pre-competitive measures envisaged by Porter, which revolve around the establishment of technology support agencies, infrastructure development and training of SMEs' entrepreneurs. The measures also imply the notion of support for industries as a whole, rather than individual industries or even individual companies.

1.5 Re-conceptualising the Role of Learning in Regional Development

There is a growing body of academic research investigating the role of learning in regional development. Storper adopts the concept of *learning economy* elaborated by the Aalborg group of economists in Denmark (Dalum *et al.*, 1992, pp. 298-317), based on two fundamental processes: technological learning and institutional learning (Storper, 1995, p. 212). Lundvall has captured the importance of this perspective, which emerged from studies of national systems of innovation. According to him, learning is the most important process, while knowledge and information are the most fundamental resources in a modern economy. He argues that 'learning is also predominantly an interactive and socially embedded process which is better understood by viewing individuals, organisations and whole societies interconnectedly in their institutional and cultural context' (Lundvall, 1992, p. 1).

Lundvall's seminal work has encouraged further contributions to the debate on how regional success is underpinned by the processes of learning and innovation (e.g. Konstadakopulos and Christopoulos, 1997). The two most recent regional growth concepts (i.e. the innovative milieu and technological change), as well as earlier ones, make strong claims about the role of the region, and agree on the following obvious factors underpinning success: agglomeration economies, economies of scope, the existence of trust, networks of SMEs, and supportive institutions. However, taking into account the previously identified shortcomings of these concepts, neither has yet given a wholly convincing explanation of the growth and technological development of regional economies. It appears that a region's ability to learn, innovate and develop new technology is conditioned by a large number of partly interdependent factors which cannot be accounted for by either concept or any other regional growth theories (Sternberg, 1996a, p. 535). Nevertheless, both concepts show how generic processes interact with historically evolved local (micro-), regional/sub-regional (meso-), and national/supranational (macro-environmental) conditions. It is the complex interactions and the collective dynamics of *geographical proximity* between economic actors, institutions, knowledge producers, disseminators and users that enable regions, localities and agglomerations to prosper or decline. Their performance depends on their efficiency, competence, flexibility, internal synergy, and external linkages.

However, according to Dupuy and Gilly, such dynamics 'cannot be achieved solely in terms of pure market logic (standard theory and institutionalist new economy); they must also integrate 'invisible' forms that support social relations such as conventions, norms, and collective knowledge' (Dupuy and Gilly, 1996, p. 1603). It is the presence of a collective order - the 'civic [political] culture' postulated by Putnam et al. (1993) - and of co-ordination that is necessary for the development of a learning economy (Storper, 1995, pp. 212-3). The essential argument here is that the regions, localities and agglomerations (and their firms) that combine social cohesion and a reasonably consistent innovation/technological policy with an openness to the rest of the world, have the best chance to learn in order to identify and adopt new trends and developments at the global level.

However, it has been acknowledged that innovations originate in many different *spheres* or *environments*. The challenge of regional development thus goes way beyond the economic relationships necessary for the creation of innovative milieux and transition pathways. Their creation requires a general attitude that Friedmann calls a *rooted cosmopolitan culture* (Friedmann, 1991, p. 177) and Kanter *cosmopolitanism* (Kanter, 1995, p. 61), both of which foster three elements: collective learning, consensus and co-ordination, by all of the relevant actors.

Morgan (1997) draws upon the works of Lundvall et al. (1992), Lundvall and Johnson (1994), and Grabher and Stark (1997) to highlight the role of learning and knowledge, and of Putnam *et al.* (1993) to emphasise the importance of the strong co-operative ethos at regional level via the concept of the *learning region*. In the context of learning regions, learning is taking place in all parts of society and includes the building of competencies, and not just access to information (Hudson, 1999).

In such a milieu, the process of learning is brought about by the activity of participating companies, research institutions (i.e. universities), government and support institutions[8], the mobility of the workforce, and the interconnections between suppliers and customers. This process is assisted by face-to-face contacts, which are aided by geographical proximity. The main assumption of the afore-mentioned GREMI group is that the innovative firm is not a predetermined entity within a local environment, but is created by this environment, with innovative behaviour dependent upon factors determined at a local or regional level.

Why then are some regions of the world more conducive to innovation than others? Regional economists argue that such variation is attributed to the specificity of milieux, which *metabolise* technologies, markets and resources in different ways, thereby opening up new and original opportunities for a region and its firms.

The milieu, therefore, comprises not only economic relationships, but also ones that are political, cultural, social and organisational. For instance, the existence of a specific political climate in combination with entrepreneurial spirit and experience of flexible production systems is more important for the economic well-being of a region than the size of its capital resources and labour market. Political, cultural, organisational and social factors (such as willingness to employ women and immigrants), which will be discussed in our final chapter, are considered more important for innovation than technology, or the region's human or physical resources.

1.6 The Exploitation of Collective Learning: An Easy and Inexpensive Way to Innovate

It should be noted that collective learning derives from the aggregate knowledge of individuals, individual firms, and institutions, and is not proprietary. As an externality within the milieu, it is absolutely free. As mentioned earlier, it is up to SMEs to absorb and exploit collective learning. In this respect, the collective learning process is seen to generate radical innovation (such as James Dyson's) rather than incremental innovation. The firm's ability to produce a radical or breakthrough innovation is based on new knowledge and scientific and managerial expertise, which stems from the historical process of cumulative know-how and learning processes. When entrepreneurs need to achieve a radical innovation, they are more likely to exploit the existence of a large pool of skilled local labour, which brings with it accumulated knowledge. For instance, James Dyson employed a team of skilled engineers, many of whom had been working previously in local defence or aerospace firms, in order to design his unique vacuum cleaner. In contrast, process innovation requires incremental innovation, and is the outcome of internal knowledge within each firm. An entrepreneur is unlikely to try to develop a new product himself if somebody else can either do it for him or in collaboration with him. According to recent findings in the Silicon Valley in California and in the Italian high-tech areas, such a company is likely to be found in high-technology SMEs' milieux characterised by a rigorous new company spin-off in which research ideas and technological innovations are shared and diffused.

> ... Silicon Valley does business differently from other places. Engineers and programmers hop from company to company, and share options stretch from the boardroom to the reception desk ... the place is a strange mixture of rampant individualism and collaboration: staff are borrowed, ideas shared, favours exchanged ...
>
> (*The Economist*, 29 March 1997)[9]

Some Cambridge academics, referring to the Cambridge and Oxford regional innovative milieux, have shown how collective learning is diffused. They note that:

> ...empirical findings reveal a high intensity of diffusion of embodied technological and research expertise via entrepreneurial spin-offs, together with a significant degree of continuing interaction and co-operation between 'parent' and spin-off firms which is likely to reflect relations of trust and a regional collective capability.

> (Keeble et al., 1997)

Geographical proximity also helps the establishment of horizontal linkages and activities between companies (particularly SMEs) across sectors and technologies. As mentioned earlier, a feedback effect takes place after the establishment of the innovative milieu which reinforces the elements of continuity in the form of a stable labour market and stable inter-SMEs' linkages, and dynamic synergies in the form of interactive mechanisms leading to innovation. Stable labour relations mean that although there is an apparent labour mobility and flexible employment within the milieu itself (i.e. skilled workers can move between firms) there is hardly any inflow or outflow of skilled workforce to destabilise it. Stable linkages imply a wide variety of arrangements, from informal personal contacts to more formal sub-contracting or cross-sharing. Interactive mechanisms imply a significant degree of continuing interaction and co-operation between groups of SMEs for the development of product innovation (Mitra, 2000). This interaction, as Lawson points out, 'is not simply (or most importantly) concerned with core research but with the more 'down stream' phase of innovation, involving detailed product design, testing, redesign and production' (Lawson, 1997, p. 23).

1.7 The Importance of Networking for SMEs

Collective learning becomes a comparative advantage of the innovative milieu, although it is also a barrier to entry into the local market, and may be transformed in the long run into a barrier to exit. However, the innovative milieu needs external contacts or *external energies* from outside the system, in terms of new technological opportunities, to avoid losing its innovative capability (Camagni, 1991, p. 140; Bramanti and Ratti, 1997, pp. 32-33; Sternberg, 2000, p. 394). The GREMI group assigns these external linkages to *innovation networks*.[10] The process of networking is taking place both at the intra-regional level, in the form of collective learning processes, and through inter-regional (or even global) linkages facilitating the firm's access to different, though localised, innovation capabilities (Konstadakopulos and Christopoulos, 1997). Therefore, technological dynamism depends on both the local and non-local innovative processes. The central link between them is the learning process: the codes, routines, interaction channels, and different ways to organise and co-ordinate learning behaviour, which make learning possible (Bramanti and Ratti, 1997). Networking is 'an effective way of tackling some of the problems that beset small companies purely on account of their size' (*Financial Times*, 28 January 1997).

However, given the complexity of networks, it is doubtful whether small firms could maintain them over the longer term (Harris et al., 2000, p. 238). Figure 1.1 depicts the innovation network of Science Systems plc, one of the sampled firms in the West of England. Actors involved in innovation are represented as nodes in the diagram. Directional relations between the actors are represented as lines between the nodes. Unfortunately, because of the need to maintain commercial confidentiality, it was not possible to establish the strength associated with each line. However, the diagram indicates the type of external actor with whom the firm's managers and engineers interact in the innovation process.

In the study of networks, the decision-making process can be analysed to show how actors relate to each other, and how their interaction can lead to co-operative solutions. There are many types of network, other than innovation networks, within which local economic actors and, in particular, firms are embedded (Sternberg, 2000, pp. 393-4; Malecki, 2002). For instance, the so-called *socio-political networks* are equally important, as they structure the relations of local economic actors and provide them with different linkages to central and supranational policy-makers. The importance of socio-political networks in structuring interactions among different individuals and groups has been explored by Granovetter (1985) and Knoke (1990), and the importance of socio-economic institutional and associative issues for regional development are discussed by Streeck and Schmitter (1991), Amin and Thrift (1995), Locke (1995), Grabher (1993), and Grabher and Stark (1997). In particular, Streeck and Schmitter suggest that a distinctive associative order, based on a guild structure, was in existence in the late medieval cities of Italy, France and Catalonia, as well as in the Rhineland and Northern Europe (Streeck and Schmitter, 1991, p. 230).

The associative order, however, is very wide and encompasses an organised civil society, co-operatives, political parties, local administration, mass membership organisations, trade associations, professional societies, and local charities. Furthermore, it is important in promoting patterns of social solidarity and local politics (Putnam 1993; Locke, 1995; Kanter, 1995; Raco, 2002). Empirical studies of the most advanced industrialised Mediterranean regions, such as Lombardy, Emilia-Romagna and Catalonia, suggest that economic development appears to benefit from the above co-operative forms of interaction and dense social networks, as well as from an outward, rather than inward, orientation (Garofoli, 1994; Locke, 1995; Picard and Konstadakopulos, 1997; Christopoulos and Konstadakopulos, 1999; Konstadakopulos, 2000a and 2000b).

In South-East Asia, Chinese business networks have been the subject of scholarly investigation by many authors (e.g. Li, 1998; Hamilton, 1998; Yeung, 1998 and 2000a). An empirical investigation by Yeung of business networks between Malaysia and Singapore (1998) reveals that there are many different types based on ethnic ties and family relationships. Such networks have been important mechanisms through which economic synergies and reciprocal investment flow between the two countries.

In conclusion, the theoretical concepts presented in this chapter illustrate that the institutional setting and local context are important determinants in promoting the innovative activities of SMEs. Context is vital in the sense that regional agglomerations, and socio-political and business networks, influence the learning behaviour and innovative capacity of firms. The next chapter, on the evolutionary development of technological policies in Europe and ASEAN in the context of the broader debate on the emerging knowledge-based economy, seeks to develop this point. Through an analysis of technological policies, it traces the way that the regional agglomerations of the West of England and the Singapore-Johor cross-border area evolved in order to produce fundamentally different types of economic development.

Figure 1.1: Science Systems plc: External Sources of Innovative Ideas

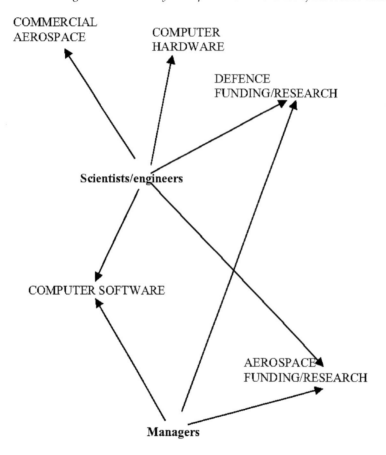

Source: UWE, (1999).

Notes

[1] For instance, *The Economist* points out that the rate of return for 17 successful innovations in America in the 1970s averaged 56%, whereas for the last 30 years the average return for all American businesses was just 16% (*The Economist*, (1999), *'A Survey of Innovation in Industry'*, 20 February).

[2] The South West of England consists of the counties and unitary authorities of Gloucestershire, South Gloucestershire, Swindon and Wiltshire, Bristol, Somerset, Bath & North East Somerset, North Somerset, Bournemouth, Dorset and Poole, Devon, Torbay and Plymouth, and Cornwall and the Isles of Scilly.

[3] For a comparative analysis of some of the regional growth theories, such as long wave theory, flexible specialisation and production, industrial districts, and locational determinants, see Sternberg, 1996a and 1996b, and Storper, 1995.

[4] See, among others, Aydalot, 1986 and 1988; Aydalot and Keeble, 1988; Camagni, 1991; Maillat 1991.

[5] Lorenzen, 2001, uses the term 'localized learning'.

[6] See, for instance, Nahm and Volderembse, 2002, for a theory of post-industrial manufacturing based on an extensive and detailed analysis of literature.

[7] However, a number of commentators warn that founding a policy exclusively on promotion of the clusters is a risky policy (RSA, 2001, p. 26; Martin, and Sunley, 2001, pp. 12-13).

[8] This is known as the 'triple helix' approach, a term coined by Etzowitz and Leyessdorff in order to analyse the wider industry-university-government relations in the context of the emerging global knowledge economy (cf. Book Review by Geuna, A., in *The Economic Journal*, 109: 456, (1999), pp. 464-467). Such relations will be examined in more detail in subsequent chapters.

[9] *The Economist*, 1997, 'A Survey of the Silicon Valley', 29 March, p. 6.

[10] For the factors that influence the organisational and spatial embeddedness of innovation networks in the Dutch region of Noord-Brabant, see Oerlemans et al., (2001).

Chapter 2:

Technological Innovation Policies in the EU and ASEAN Economies

2.1 The Emerging Global Knowledge Economy

In the previous chapter we looked at the importance of learning for innovation in the context of the innovative milieu. However, it is useful to bear in mind the difference between learning and knowledge: learning is a process, while knowledge is a resource. In this chapter, we place the process of learning in the context of the so-called knowledge-based economy. We consider how the forces of globalisation of economic activity and the advancement of technology point to the advent of knowledge as a source of economic growth and societal development. If we can identify the determinants which influence decision-makers and corporate management to adopt technological innovation policies and strategies leading to a knowledge-based economy, we can begin to understand the extent to which EU-ASEAN technological co-operation could be advanced.

It is now widely acknowledged that the world's developed economies, and increasingly those that are still developing, are more dependent on the production, dissemination and utilisation of knowledge than ever before. Both governments and firms are spending more and more resources on the production of knowledge. Investment in knowledge (R&D, software, and public and private spending in education and training) exceeds 10% of OECD-wide GDP (OECD, 1999, p. 7). Embodied in human capital and technology, it is creating new industries and services, such as information technology, telecommunications, multimedia, biotechnology, and advanced materials, and is encouraging the emergence and growth of new knowledge-intensive firms. However, the knowledge-based economy is developing in an era of profound changes in the world economy. The liberalisation of markets for goods and services, financial market reforms and new technological opportunities has increased the importance of knowledge. Technology and the globalisation of markets are also freeing firms from their historic roots. As firms reorganise their activities globally, governments are becoming concerned about devising new technological policies to foster the production, use and diffusion of knowledge.

This last point is of particular importance. During the last few years a new paradigm of promoting the knowledge-based economy has emerged, in which investment in science and technology, improvement in educational provision, the creation of a skilled and flexible workforce, and support for technology-based exports are of paramount importance. Moreover, the development of such an economy requires the adoption of a clear vision to give focus and priority to socio-economic policy actions designed and implemented at the national, and increasingly the sub-national and supranational, level. Although the knowledge-based economy has surfaced as an important issue in Europe and South-East Asia, we know relatively little about it. However, animated discussion on its implications has already started to develop (Castells, 1996; OECD, 1996, 1999 and 2001; Leadbeater, 1999; Thurow, 1999; Kuklinski and Orlowski, 2000; Kuklinski, 2000a; RSA, 2001).

It seems to be the case that the increasing integration of international and European industrial systems into three main trading blocs (the EU, ASEAN and the North Atlantic Free Trade Agreement area), as well as the growing importance of regional and urban agglomerations, is affecting the emergence of the knowledge-based economy. The question is, to what extent does such integration facilitate a greater than ever flow of goods, services and investment, as well as the exchange of tacit and codified technological knowledge? Fortunately, the literature refers to many examples of successful stories from regions around the world that are centres of knowledge and innovation. For instance, the computing industry of California's Silicon Valley (Hall, 1997), the clustering of biotechnology firms in the Cambridge area of the United Kingdom (Cooke, 2002), and the concentration of biomedical equipment and software firms in Dublin indicate that such regional agglomerations are important examples of the emerging knowledge-based economy.

The regional dimension is important because, as mentioned in the previous chapter, geographical proximity is a significant element in the process of learning for innovation, and therefore the territorial attachment of knowledge. As we shall see later, the West of England sub-region - part of the administrative region of the South West of England - is also acquiring a specialisation in knowledge-intensive sectors, such as aerospace, multimedia and precision engineering, especially in the so-called *golden triangle* of Bristol, Swindon and Cheltenham. Matthiessen and Schwarz, in their analysis of research strength and patterns of specialisation based on bibliometric indicators, rank the urban agglomeration of Bristol - jointly with that of Cardiff, in neighbouring South Wales - an outstanding centre of knowledge in Europe. It is placed fifth after Cambridge, Oxford-Reading, Geneva-Lausanne and Basel-Mulhouse-Freiburg (Matthiessen and Schwarz, 2000, pp. 53-55).

South-East Asia, too, has attracted attention, especially the *growth triangle* of Singapore, Johor (Malaysia) and Riau (Indonesia). The so-called *SIJORI triangle* is one of the most important high-technology agglomerations in South-East Asia (Tang and Thant, 1994; Lim, 1996; Low, 1998; Debrah et al., 2000). The triangle - a trilateral co-operation arrangement taking place between Singapore, the southern-most part of the Malaysian State of Johor, and the nearby Indonesian islands of Bintan and Batam (part of the Riau province) - is developing capabilities not only to serve trans-national corporations (TNCs) but also to nurture local knowledge-based enterprises.

It is suggested that the economic dynamics and organisation of the growth triangles, industrial districts and innovative milieux can be best understood in the wider context of social relationships among firms, and between firms and knowledge institutions in their geographical clusters. A particularly important feature of this assertion is the suggestion that the social and organisational structure of regional agglomerations generates a *market culture* in which economic decisions and activities take place (Konstadakopulos, 2001). Although the focus of this work is the way in which small innovative and knowledge-intensive firms learn to innovate, we shall also look at how policy-makers and company managers of such firms are preparing themselves for the emerging knowledge-based economy in the 21st century. In this and the final chapter, we examine the relevance of the economic, political and social environment in shaping markets and learning behaviours in the two high-technology regional agglomerations of the West of England and the Singapore-Johor cross-border area. The term *region* is used in its generic sense, meaning a geographical area rather than an administrative region. Since we are looking at the effect of specific market cultures on the development of small knowledge-intensive firms, the origins and evolution of technology policies at supranational, national and regional level are instructive. It is also important to consider additional factors, such as cultural differences, local entrepreneurial practices and attitudes, and the existence of trust in the respective regional politico-administrative settings that encourage inter-organisational collaboration and knowledge acquisition. In the final part of this chapter, the implications of technology policies that have developed in response to the emerging knowledge-based economy are analysed in the light of EU-ASEAN technological co-operation.

2.2 The Evolutionary Development of Technological Policy in Europe

Macroeconomic factors in Europe have undoubtedly influenced the performance of all its regions. These regions have been affected by a wide range of policy areas, a key one being industrial policy, which includes elements such as assistance for innovation and R&D, and diffusion of new technology. The manufacture of new products and the development and diffusion of new production and organisational processes are central to the competitiveness of both national and regional economies. Governments, development agencies and supranational institutions, such as the EU, ASEAN, the World Bank and OECD, have become involved at all spatial levels in seeking to stimulate innovation.

In the continuing effort to generate economic growth in Europe, as well as to reduce regional disparities, few issues have received more attention than the phenomenon of technological innovation. There seems to be a long-standing interest in the problems of *peripheral* and technologically weak regions in contrast to *core* and technologically strong regions, and these problems have been exacerbated by the process of European integration. Naturally, technological innovation manifests itself differently in the various European regions, depending on the region's industrial structure, as well as socio-political and cultural conditions (Konstadakopulos, 2000a). The legacy of historical tradition is also important in understanding how the technological innovation policy process has evolved over time, and how it is structured in order to suit varying local conditions. Primarily, an important element in the development of technology policy has been the recognition that technology, as an autonomous policy area in the form of public intervention policy, can play a crucial role in regional economic development. In Europe, this began to take place after the Second World War with the rise of specialised research and development, and with the emergence of large R&D projects associated with the development of new weapons and defence systems. Apart from these large R&D projects, the main mechanism for strengthening technological innovation since the second half of the twentieth century has been the promotion of economic growth.

According to Caraça, the post-war era is divided into three different periods (Caraça, 1997). The first period ended in the late 1960s and corresponded to the post-war economic reconstruction of Europe. The main technology policies adopted by the majority of European countries during the 1950s and 1960s were directed towards increasing the level of basic research, and aimed at the setting up of strategic sectors in the economy necessary for supporting economic growth. One important development of the 1950s and 1960s was the establishment of research councils, national R&D laboratories and other scientific institutions, which clearly promoted innovation and economic growth. The rather simplistic *linear model of innovation* prevailed (Freeman, 1995, p. 9), founded on formal knowledge generated by basic R&D activity, large firms and *national systems of innovation* (Asheim, 1997). A characteristic of these national systems was that they had their own distinctive approaches to policy. However, the direction of policies was influenced to a great extent by common European geo-strategic, economic and financial considerations in relation to the Cold War and the emergence of the three European Economic Communities (later known as the European Community). Most importantly, the generation and diffusion of technological innovation became a topic of regional analysis in the 1950s and 1960s, particularly with the growth pole theory, the diffusion theory, the product cycle and the filtering down approaches.[1]

However, in the second period - the 1970s and early 1980s - new distinctive technology policies emerged, partly in response to the challenge of technologically advanced American and Japanese multinationals. The majority of national governments in Europe devised their own systems of industrial policy, but with a new focus on restructuring traditional industries and developing those they considered of strategic importance, especially in high-technology sectors. This was the technocratic policy of *national champions*, adopted mainly by France and the UK but also by other European countries.

One interesting aspect of the situation in Europe at that time was the rapid expansion of the higher education system. Education was one of the main catalysts that transformed the relationship between science and technology and the economy. In addition, comprehensive technological innovation policies emerged for the first time, towards the end of this period (Caraça, 1997). As we shall see in more detail in the next section, a more specific pressure, in the form of a bottom-up regionalism, started to emerge in the unitary European states during the late 1970s. In Italy and Spain, this resulted in the establishment of regional institutions, which began to develop their own regional policies. In France, the regionalisation process was much slower, resulting in 1986 in the creation of elected regions, while in the UK the process of devolution of technology policies to the regions is still an on-going process. However, the decentralisation of regional policies has not been limited to a mere transfer of power from central government to the regions, but also to the creation of a wide range of support measures, the provision of funds, and market-orientated initiatives. Since the 1980s, regional policy in Europe, in which technological innovation is central, has targeted projects that foster regional competitiveness, reduce regional disparities and promote product or process innovation and diffusion of technology.

In the third period - the late 1980s and the 90s - the predominant discourse was concerned with the issues of European integration and the globalisation of the economy, as well as the growing significance of technological innovation for international competitiveness. We have observed that regional forms of governance, and consequently regional technology policies, started to emerge during the 1980s. One interesting aspect of this development is the fact that national technology policies in Europe also began to evolve during this period, in order to accommodate the structural changes across industries and firms. The mission-orientated nature of supporting strategic sectors and national champions of technological policy, practised by countries such as the UK and France, gave way to a more diffusion-orientated one, adopted by Germany, which aimed at enhancing knowledge diffusion and technology transfer. Policy tools currently in use are tax credits, subsidies, the intellectual property system, enhanced research productivity, and competition policy (Eaton et al., 1998; Hall, 2002). However, the regional impact of national technology policies was not considered at the time. While there have clearly been constraints on the functioning of regional innovation systems (Cooke et al., 2000, pp. 134-5), they are now becoming a very important part of the overall system, especially in federal, and to some extent quasi-federal, states (Heijs, 1997). Moreover, in the late 1990s there was a shift in the national policies of EU member states from concern about regional disparities to the need to comply with the EMU criteria and promote national competitiveness at an international level (Soete, 2001, p. 145).

2.2.1 Policy Patterns in European Regional Agglomerations

In the European Union, profound changes are currently taking place in the context of European integration. These developments are associated with structural changes in economic activity, technological progress, new forms of business organisations, and an increased awareness of the existence of common territorial spaces within neighbouring localities and regions. The regions of the EU, however defined[2], are becoming powerful political and economic actors, assuming a proactive and dynamic economic and political role. This is seen in political mobilisation of regions and the dynamism of regional economies. However, a strong divergence exists between the various European regions, not only in terms of economic growth but also in culture, governance, and political and social orientation.

The essence of this section is the assumption that economic restructuring in Europe is leading both to an ever-growing integration of national economies and to the increasing importance of the regions as competitive units. This can be observed in forms of behaviour in some trade patterns and regional and inter-regional initiatives. Increasingly, the European regions are involved in building intra-regional networks and collaborative cross-border relations. Thus, an inter-regional form of mobilisation has emerged, involving the creation of transnational bodies and groupings, and a system of international representation that has made some regions important actors in Europe. In addition, regional and local entities, driven by the realisation of the single European market and reinforced by the on-going process of European Monetary Union, are adopting economic policies with a view to competing in the wider international context of economic globalisation. Therefore, increasing territorial competition - mainly to attract inward investment - is taking place between members of the European Union and their regions. The process of regionalisation has considerably enhanced territorial competition by de-concentration and decentralisation of economic policies. The various institutional arrangements and forms of political mobilisation taking place across Europe have introduced modes of interaction that include both territorial competition and territorial collaboration. It is important, therefore, to analyse this paradox of regional collaboration and competition, and understand how these new forms of behaviour could help the economic restructuring and political integration of the European regions, as well as determine what part national states and the EU play.

The emergence of regions is a relatively new phenomenon in Europe. With the exception of federal Germany, regional institutions either did not exist or, if they did, lacked power and resources of their own. Regional policy was designed - and in most cases implemented - by central governments. Nevertheless, during the late 1970s a more specific pressure in the form of a bottom-up regionalism started to emerge. This coincided with the increase of regional identities and the revival of interest in minority languages and cultures. At the same time, regional institutions in Europe started to develop into elected regional governments, with more influence on the development of regional policies. In Italy this happened as early as the 1970s. The Italian model was followed by Spain, which in its 1978 constitution created seventeen autonomous communities. In France, because of the strong state, the regionalisation process was much slower than in Spain, and elected regions only came into existence in 1986. In contrast, Belgium - which can be described as a weak state - was quick to adopt a functional system of federalism. In Greece, administrative regions were introduced in the late 1980s, but they have only recently started to play a role in regional policy. More recently, regional autonomy was granted to Scotland, Wales, Northern Ireland and London, while the English regions were only permitted to establish regional development agencies and non-elected regional chambers. Now, in the early 21st century, the majority of the EU member states have some kind of regional government and, by implication, some kind of regional policy. Moreover, technology policy is moving closer to the centre of such regional policy (Vence et al., 2000).

Regionalism in Europe has set free forces beyond the control of any nation state. It is affecting the restructuring of political relationships, and generating new political issues. On a higher level, the EU has acquired more powers over trade and economic policies, and is exerting a greater influence on the world stage than its individual member nations would have without its existence. In addition, the EU's single European market and European Monetary Union have changed the nature of relationships between the three different levels of governance: supranational, national and sub-national. For instance, the *Washington Post*, reporting on the emergence of European regions, noted that 'Europe's political and economic landscape is undergoing a quiet revolution, as national governments find they are too big to manage the problems of daily life but too small to handle many global crises' (*Washington Post*, 22 October 1995).

There is also evidence that, in the single European market, business decisions that are shaping Europe's destiny are being made on the basis of regional rather than national policies. Firms are much more concerned about local tax breaks, human resources and geographical proximity to markets, when they decide to invest in new plant facilities (De Bernardy, 1999, p. 349; Yeung et al., 2001, pp. 159-161). Therefore, a new generation of policy-makers is focusing on giving greater powers to the regions and localities (Viesti, 2002, p. 474). The devolution of power downward, and the resulting decentralisation of regional policies, is correlated to a number of EU initiatives.

A central goal of the EU is to attempt to develop a co-ordinated approach to regional development processes and regional socio-economic problems on a large, regional scale, taking into account specific regional problems. European regional policy, co-ordinated by the European Commission's DGXVI, brought many actions aimed at addressing disparities between regions. *Europe 2000* and *Europe 2000+* are two important initiatives analysing spatial development trends on a transnational and European scale. The European Commission has been trying for some time to promote regional innovation and trans-European transport networks. The former has two dimensions: the networking of sectors of technological excellence between regions, and the broadening of structures of technological dissemination, especially for SMEs. In the transport sector, efforts are aimed at increasing co-operation projects between modes of transport and the promotion of inter-regional transport links. Cross-border co-operation initiatives, such as *INTERREG* and the more recent *European Regional Development Fund (ERDF) Article 10* programme, are specifically targeted at transnational co-operation in spatial planning. Actions on innovation, for instance, are funded by the *Structural Funds,* and particularly by their policy instrument, namely the *ERDF,* the principal source of finance in the Community for regional development, innovation and technology transfer.

Since 1988, the Structural Funds have made obligatory the use of *partnership,* an institutional mechanism that injects a greater degree of responsibility into regional policy by bringing the region or relevant sub-national authority into the policy process. Moreover, the ERDF specifically aims at encouraging co-operation and the exchange of experience between regional and local authorities involved with regional development. Projects funded by the Structural Funds include a variety of initiatives with a regional dimension. The most important ones related to economic development and technological innovation are: integration of the peripheral regional economies into the international and European economies; the development of technological research through co-operation; the development of internal resources; and the promotion of training.

Notwithstanding the involvement of the EU, the regionalisation of policy delivery has resulted in a number of benefits which derive from greater knowledge of relevant characteristics of local economy and policy networks. Experts in regional economic development indicate that one of the determinants of the international competitiveness of European and other world regions is their ability to exploit external economies of scale in innovation (Camagni, 1991 and 1995), as well as to accumulate social capital in the form of 'traditions of co-operation' (Storper, 1993 and 1995) and associationism (Amin and Thrift, 1995; Locke, 1995; Seely Brown and Duguid, 2000).

There are some regions and cities that act as poles of excellence and knowledge, where the most innovative ideas can be developed, making them a centre of economic activity (Matthiessen and Schwarz, 2000; Lever, 2002; Howells, 2002). An important element here is the interaction of coalitions of political, economic, cultural and social actors devoted to economic development in a specific region. Increasingly, regional policy is made and formulated within socio-political networks. Potential actors include the regional and local institutions, the central state, the EU and economic interests. It is through the interaction of these institutions within a given context that intra- or inter-regional collaboration and/or territorial competition are defined and take place. Active participation across economy, state and civil society is considered to be the basis for generating economic success, making it more democratically accountable by producing a political process which is more locally responsive (Amin and Thrift, 1995). However, central government policies still continue to influence the structure of opportunities available to regional systems, and state agencies may be directly involved in regional level policies. Therefore, the regionalisation of policies can only be partial, not total (Konstadakopulos et al., 1998), especially in non-federal member states.

The development of the European Union and its forthcoming enlargement undeniably affects social, political and economic configurations within each member state. In the light of these developments, policy-making has shifted away from national administrators up to the supranational level and down to the sub-national level (regional or local) (Eser and Konstadakopulos, 2000). In the late 1980s, many of the European regions came together to create two lobbying groups, the Assembly of European Regions and the Conference of European Maritime Peripheral Regions. This institutional evolution was intensified in 1993 by the creation of the Committee of the Regions (CoR), through the Treaty of Maastricht. In addition, the Treaty of Amsterdam, which came into force on 1st May 1999, reinforced the position of the CoR in the EU decision-making process, by granting, for the first time, the right of consultation to the European Parliament. This regionalisation of Europe has been matched by the progressive rise of new transnational groupings such as the *Euroregions* and the city networks. The above examples illustrate a general tendency towards regional mobilisation, and the importance of the European framework in which regional and technological policies now take place.

However, the European regions are responding differently to the challenges of international competition and European integration, as are their sectors of industry.

What we are now witnessing is not just the Europeanisation of the regions' economic activity, but more importantly their internationalisation.

2.2.2 The Industrial District of the West of England

The West of England is the north-eastern part of the administrative region of the South West of England[3], one of the UK's largest. In order to understand the specificities of this sub-region, it is necessary to examine the political economy of the South West as a whole. Although the South West is a peripheral region, it has been growing faster than any other region in England. It also performs well in a European context when compared with regions of similar size and industrial structure. Its Gross Domestic Product (GDP) is only 95% of the EU average, but displays high levels of economic activity (61% compared to the EU average of 55%) (SWERDA, 2000). However, there is extreme divergence in the region, with the county of Wiltshire in the east having a GDP of 115% compared to only 70% in the extreme south-western county of Cornwall. The economy of the South West is not particularly dependent on foreign investment, as the number of foreign-owned companies is smaller than in most other British regions. Nevertheless, it has been a favourite location of inward investment, and over 1,200 companies that are foreign-controlled - mostly of American or Far Eastern origin - are now situated in the region. The main incentives for relocation in the South West are considered to be the English language [and culture], and accessibility to the EU's markets[4]. As mentioned in the introduction, the region has a relatively large number of indigenous SMEs and a strong culture of entrepreneurship. Only a small proportion of its workforce is engaged in manufacturing, and this sector is not concentrated in traditional heavy industries. The best performing sectors in the region are aerospace, financial services, and electronics.

During the 1970s and early 1980s, the central government in London, through the Government Office for the South West, pursued economic development policies by focusing on attracting high technology to the region. During that period, the Department of Trade and Industry provided high-technology grants, especially to the large electronics and defence and aerospace companies, whose R&D departments happened to be situated largely in the South West of England. However, in the late 1980s, the Conservative government adopted more sophisticated policies, which sought to improve technology transfer and the technological performance of indigenous firms. During that time the central government reduced R&D grant aid and launched instead a number of regionalised technology transfer initiatives.

In the 1990s, subsidies in support of technology and innovation were reduced further, partly in order to comply with the EU's competition legislation. Such support was only made available for pre-competitive research within SMEs with the adoption of the following programmes: the *LINK* scheme assists companies, particularly SMEs, to undertake joint research with higher educational institutions; the *Advanced Technology Programmes* seek to promote long-term collaboration between UK companies working in advanced technologies; and the *General Industrial Collaborative Projects* programme of the early 1990s sought to bring together companies for collaboration, particularly small ones and research institutions. The British Government still offers two nationwide schemes - introduced in 1991 - in support of single-company innovation projects, which are seen as an exception to the collaborative rule: *SMART* and *SPUR*. In addition, small firms in Assisted Areas, EU Objective 2 Areas and certain urban areas could receive the *Regional Enterprise Grant for Innovation Projects (RIG)*. However, surveys and analyses of the innovative performance of Scottish manufacturing (Ashcroft et al., 1995) and of companies situated in the South West of England (Konstadakopulos, 1997) suggest that the most recent UK innovation policy has been largely irrelevant or at least insignificant. Since 1997, the Labour government's so-called 'New Regional Policy' has focused on supply-side improvements for the enhancement of competitiveness, through science and technology. Such thinking is based on the 'new growth' theoretical concept - a concept which is in fact a 'subtle re-working' of policies adopted by the Conservative government in the 1980s (RSA, 2001, pp. 13-14). The New Regional Policy favours long-term macroeconomic stability and growth of certain areas of the national and regional economy.

However, it is important to mention that, prior to the creation of the Regional Development Agency in 1999, the majority of the regional technology initiatives were unfocused, uncoordinated, contradictory and fragmentary (Konstadakopulos, 2000a). Nevertheless, the plethora of policy agents in the region, including the Regional Development Agency, intermediary development partnerships, business support organisations and technology-orientated research institutions, are now focusing on networks and supply chains for the diffusion of technology, rather than just on individual companies or narrowly defined industries.

The beginnings of the aerospace and electronics sectors in the South West of England - in which British high-technology industry has been internationally successful - can be traced back to the post-war years. It was mainly as a result of public procurement policies that national companies were favoured by the Ministry of Defence. It was also the industrial policy of the Labour government in the 1960s and 70s that assisted the establishment of many high-technology companies in the region. Today, the region has divisions of the most important British/European aerospace and defence companies, such as BAe, GKN-Westland, Messier-Dowty and Rolls Royce, and many of their principal suppliers and subcontractors. As mentioned earlier, a number of American high-technology electronic companies (such as Dupont Electronics, Hewlett Packard, Intel, Logica, Lucent Technologies and Motorola) came to the West of England in the late 1970s and 80s, and built plants within the M4 corridor, thereby giving them easy access to London and Heathrow Airport. Japanese (e.g. Honda) and European (mainly French and German) high-technology multinationals soon followed. Although many of the high-technology plants were initially production operations, or regional sales and servicing centres without significant R&D activity, this situation has now changed. Many of the high-technology TNCs have started to establish research laboratories alongside their production plants, and have begun to come into contact with regional research institutions and local firms.

The most important outcome of the high-technology clustering of TNCs and of

British aerospace and defence along the M4 corridor, and more recently along the M5, is the opportunities it provides for innovation and creativity. These are realised through technology spillovers, information sharing, and exchange of tacit and codified knowledge (Lawson and Lorenz, 1999; Mitra, 2000; Howells, 2002). As a consequence, new patterns of innovative activities have sprung up around the M4 and M5 corridors between the major urban centres of Bristol, Cheltenham and Swindon. This triangle, also so-called the *Silicon Gorge*, exhibits a knowledge-based economy characterised by the establishment of innovative and knowledge-intensive firms and knowledge institutions. In addition, a new type of firm and a new market culture is emerging in the knowledge-driven sectors of the local economy. Indigenous companies in consumer electrical products (e.g. Dyson Ltd., the most celebrated innovator in the region, mentioned in chapter 1), multimedia (e.g. the Oscar-winning Aardman Animations), precision engineering (e.g. Renishaw plc), and bespoke software (e.g. Science Systems plc) are already on the way to becoming large multinationals. These companies are not only firmly embedded in the region, but also have a long history of innovation, particularly in high technology. In addition, they take advantage of the region's highly skilled and educated workforce. The South West has fourteen universities and over forty colleges, and 49 per cent of all economically active adults are qualified to at least NVQ level 3 or equivalent (National Statistics, 2002).

Unlike the newly devolved Scotland, Wales, Northern Ireland and Greater London, the region does not yet possess an elected parliament or assembly. However, the South West Regional Development Agency was the first in England to launch a technology strategy for the promotion of knowledge-based industries (October 1999). The Agency, responsible for an area with a population of five million and with a modest annual budget of £92 million (2001-02), is proceeding with the implementation of its strategy. It is aiming, rather ambitiously, to promote seven sectors with the greatest potential for the region's economy, and to encourage the development of three additional ones (SWERDA, 2000). The main sectors are:

* Advanced Engineering
* Customers Marketing Services
* Environmental Technologies
* Food and Drink
* Information and Communication Technologies
* Leisure and Tourism
* Marine Technologies

The sectors to be developed are:

* Biotechnology
* Financial Services
* Printing and Packaging

The adoption of cluster policies and initiatives are important for formatting the knowledge-based economy, but in the South West of England attention was paid to these policies have only been taken seriously during the last few years (Konstadakopulos et al., 2000). As we note in the following section, the Singaporean and Malaysian governments have adopted similar policies and initiatives in order to develop their own knowledge-driven industries.

2.3 The Evolving Nature of Technological Policy in ASEAN

ASEAN is now regarded as an important regional grouping in the world economy. It is similar in many ways to its distant but important trading partner, the European Union, and consists of a group of ten highly heterogeneous member states (Brunei, Indonesia, Laos, Malaysia, Myanmar, the Philippines, Singapore, Thailand, Vietnam, and the recently admitted Cambodia; East Timor may also become a member). What is striking about ASEAN member states is their diversity in terms of economic development, political systems and population. There is a mixture of affluent and poor countries, liberal and quasi-liberal democracies, communist regimes and a military junta, and populations ranging from a few hundred thousand to almost 200 million. Despite the diversity of its make-up, however, ASEAN has begun to exert a considerable influence on world trade negotiations, although it has failed to create a genuine common market like the EU.

ASEAN member states do not trade between themselves to the same degree as EU countries, the one notable exception being Singapore and Malaysia, representing one fifth of the exports of each country (Selover, 1999, p. 238). To a lesser extent Thai trade with Singapore and Malaysia is significant, as well as Indonesian exports to Singapore. Nevertheless, between 1975 and 1996, ASEAN's intra-regional trade as a share of its total trade increased rapidly from 30% to 49% (Thornton and Goglio, 2002, p. 205). In general terms, intra-regional trade concentrates on manufacturing goods (see Figure 2.1), and accounts for less than a fifth of ASEAN trade, compared to well over 50% for the EU (Yeung et al., 1999, p. 53). One of the main reasons for the low level of intra-regional trade has been the insufficient progress made in tariff reductions. Nevertheless, ASEAN's members have agreed to create a regional free trade area (AFTA) by lowering tariffs on agricultural and industrial products to between zero and 5 per cent by 2003. The launch of AFTA, seen as an attempt to capture potential gains from intra-regional trade, has not been very successful, however. The problem has been the deeply rooted protectionist mentality of some of the members. More recently, ASEAN foreign ministers were forced to allow Malaysia an exemption from lowering tariffs on automotive trade because it threatened to quit the association's free trade agreement (*Financial Times*, 26 July 2000)[5]. However, as the ASEAN economies evolve and become specialised, intra-regional trade is likely to expand (Yeung et al., 1999, p. 54; Mursed, 2001, pp. 105-6).

Along with the rest of Asia, South-East Asian economies were engulfed by the 1997-98 financial crisis. Sharp declines in inter-regional trade, tourism and financial activity slowed down the economies of even the most thriving members of ASEAN. The crisis was a powerful shock, given the fact that in the preceding years economies throughout

Figure 2.1: Intra-ASEAN Exports

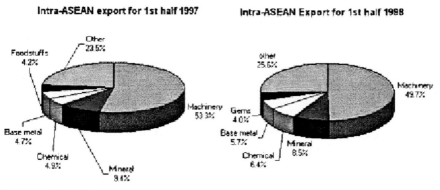

Source: ASEAN

the region had been expanding at the impressive rate of 5 to 8 per cent per annum. After a 4 per cent growth in 1997, the region contracted by about 7 per cent the following year (Asian Development Bank, 1999). However, the crisis quickly came to an end, and in 1999 the region recovered, with an average growth of about 3.4 per cent (*The Economist*, 12 February 2000)[6], although in the past two years it has been affected by the slowdown of the American economy (heightened by the events of 11 September 2001). Nevertheless, the unprecedented growth of some of the ASEAN economies has led to the creation of substantial domestic markets with high standards of living.

A close examination of the industrial policies of ASEAN countries reveals two important common features that are particularly apparent in both Singapore and Malaysia. Policies in these two countries are aimed towards R&D and technology transfer, development of strategic industries, formation of industrial clusters and the pursuance of regional networking activities (Masuyama, 1997, p. 11; EDB, 1999; Economic Planning Unit, 2001). Both countries have placed a strong emphasis on vocational courses directed towards company needs, particularly for high-technology TNCs, and are adopting policies for the development, adaptation and retraining of their workforce. These policies are paying off. According to the so-called technological ladder hypothesis postulated by Tan, it appears that Malaysia (together with Thailand and Indonesia) is the candidate most likely to join the ranks of newly industrialised countries, of which Singapore is one of the most recent members (Tan, 1996, pp. 113-115; Simandjuntak, 1998, pp. 93-94; Reynolds, 2001, p. 78).

The following sections offer a brief analysis of both Singapore and Malaysia in terms of how they are developing their own innovation systems. The two countries are undergoing major structural changes and becoming increasingly interdependent. Singapore is one of the most important investors in Malaysia, while Malaysia, with its natural resources and low-cost human capital, is influencing the industrial restructuring of Singapore (Yeung, 1998, pp. 688-689).

2.3.1 Singapore: Building a Capacity for Learning

Singapore, with its population of 3.1 million, is one of the world's smallest countries, and yet it is the most dynamic economy in the ASEAN region and the most globalised economy in the world (Hobson and Ramesh, 2002, p. 5). The small city-state, which covers an area of only 100 square kilometres, has exerted considerable influence in the political domain of the Asia-Pacific region, as well as in the rest of the world - an influence that is quite disproportionate to its size (Koh, 1998). However, political relations with its most immediate neighbours, Malaysia and Indonesia, have not always been cordial. Furthermore, Singapore's socio-political model of governance is at odds with the Western model of liberal democracy (Leifer, 1998, pp. 19-20). For instance, in the third Asia-Europe Meeting (ASEM) in Seoul in October 2000, Singapore opposed moves by European governments to include human rights and democracy in their joint declaration, calling it interference in internal affairs (*The Straits Times*, 20 October 2000)[7].

Singapore's greatest economic accomplishment is the integration and international orientation of its economy, which is mainly dependent on the performance of its expanding high-technology sector and booming services sector. A cluster of electronic industries has developed since the late 1970s, and reflects Singapore's regional role as a manufacturing base favoured by foreign TNCs (Hobday, 1997, p. 140). The electronic industry accounts for almost half of the total manufacturing output, and more than 70% of the electronic sector's exports go to the US and Europe (Chia, 1997). In contrast to its three main Asian competitors (Hong Kong, South Korea and Taiwan), indigenous companies have played a limited role in the growth of Singapore's electronic industry, as it is dominated by TNCs, although this is gradually changing. The TNCs not only enabled Singapore to export but also to acquire technological knowledge, by transferring technology to their local subsidiaries and training the local workforce. However, since 1997 the electronic industry has been adversely affected, firstly by the regional financial crisis, secondly by a global over-capacity of semiconductors and disk drives, and thirdly, and most recently, by reduced demand from the United States, due to the slowdown of its economy. The other two important industrial clusters found in Singapore - those of the chemical and pharmaceutical sectors - have not been affected, because the majority of exports are destined for the OECD countries.

Singapore now enjoys the reputation of being an exceptionally successful country, partly due to a well-managed public relations exercise, and partly to its strategic advantage of being a regional hub in South-East Asia since the early 19th century, during the British colonial rule. It is a good example to other Third World countries affected by the forces of globalisation, in the way that it has learned to attract TNCs in both manufacturing and services. The majority of such TNCs came to Singapore during the 1960s and 1970s. They were attracted by incentives to manufacturers, as well as by the political stability, disciplined workforce, strategic location, and efficient transportation and communications infrastructure. European TNCs were the first to become established in the area. For instance, Philips - one of the largest employers -

located in Singapore in 1951. The first semiconductor plant was set up in 1967 by the American company Texas Instrument, and was followed by other electronics firms.

In the 1970s, the Singapore Economic Development Board (EDB) adopted a high-technology policy, and initiated an organised campaign to attract skilled-intensive and higher valued-added export industries. This policy was intensified in the early 1980s, with the aim of attracting technology-intensive manufacturing. In 1990, the government announced the formulation of a *Strategic Economic Plan*, which became specific implementation programme initiatives by the year 2000. These initiatives are: *Manufacturing 2000*, intended to sustain manufacturing's share of GDP at more than 25%, based on the belief that it is still an important sector for an advanced economy; *International Business Hub*, aimed at enhancing Singapore's position as a business services centre for South-East Asia; *Regionalisation 2000*, which co-invests and co-manages large-scale industrial parks in partnership with national or regional authorities in Indonesia, India, China and Vietnam; *National Technology Plan*, which aims to develop Singapore into a centre of excellence in selected fields of science and technology through the intensification of R&D activity and the promotion of the indigenous innovative capability of local universities, public research institutes, and local firms[8]; *IT2000 Vision and National Information Infrastructure Initiative*, intended to exploit information technology and the development of advanced telecommunications and information infrastructures; *Local Enterprises 2000*, which aims to promote local firms by offering various inducements such as grants, preferential loans and tax incentives[9]; and the *Industry Cluster Fund*, possibly a consequence of Porter's influential stance on promoting integrated industry clusters, and aimed at investing in the development of specific industry clusters. It is not the intention here to evaluate the success of the above policies, although it should be noted that some initiatives, such as *Regionalisation 2000* - which involves the establishment of a jointly managed industrial park in China - have been problematic.

Despite the cyclical recessions of 1974-75, 1985-86 and 1997-98, and the slowdown of the economy in 2001-02, Singapore has built a modern high-technology industry and an advanced telecommunications and transport infrastructure. The city-state is now a major operational headquarters, and a logistics distribution and media/telecommunications hub for the Asia-Pacific region. The economic strategy of the government is outlined in its EDB publication *Growing a Knowledge-based Economy* (EDB, 1999). According to the Board, the main objective is to ensure that Singapore remains a highly attractive location for inward investment, and that assistance to indigenous companies continues. The vision for the next phase of development is to make Singapore a global hub of the knowledge-based economy. It is devising sectoral policies for sustaining and building on its manufacturing and services sectors, with strong emphasis on technology and innovation.

There is a striking similarity between the policies of Singapore and those of the South West of England. Like its counterpart, the Regional Development Agency, the EDB has introduced schemes to encourage companies to undertake innovation, and to upgrade and develop the skills of the workforce through its *Skills Redevelopment Programme*. The intention is also to build a modern infrastructure for the growth industries of the future. For instance, the government is developing Singapore ONE, an island-wide broadband network for delivery of interactive multimedia applications and services to businesses, schools and homes throughout the city-state.

Most importantly, Singapore is undertaking further economic liberalisation, which is necessary to persuade TNCs to locate more of their key knowledge-intensive activities locally. At the same time, it is encouraging its indigenous companies to undertake more such activities. Nevertheless, Singapore cannot yet claim to be an R&D hub. Although it is well ahead of the rest of ASEAN in this respect, it is still a net importer of technology and has not developed a strong domestic R&D capability (Jones and Lall, 1998). The latest available statistics show that R&D was only 1.13% of GNP for the 1987-97 period. This is less than half of that in both the US (2.63) and Germany (2.41) (World Bank, 2001), suggesting that Singapore has a long way to go before it can rival the technological capability of developed countries. However, in attempting to measure Singapore's progress towards a knowledge-based economy, it is clear that a great deal has been achieved. Statistics suggest that in 1998 Singapore had 458 personal computers per 1,000 inhabitants - exactly the same as the US, and well above Germany (305) and the UK (263) (World Bank, 2000).

2.3.2 Malaysia's Technological Development

Since independence in 1957, Malaysia has transformed itself from a country dependent on commodity exports into a rapidly growing economy based on manufacturing and trade. This transformation has been the result of a period of import-substitution industrialisation that led to the emergence of industrial development. Hopes of establishing a common market with Singapore were dashed, however, when Singapore was expelled from the Malay Federation in 1965. Five years later, Malaysia introduced its New Economic Policy, and then the *First Outline Perspective Plan* in 1971. During that period, policies changed from promoting import-substitution to export-orientated industries (Khalafalla and Webb, 2001, p. 1704). A regulatory measure - the controversial *Industrial Co-ordination Act* - was also introduced, aimed at encouraging participation in manufacturing by the *Bumiputra* (indigenous Malays), who were perceived to be at a disadvantage compared with the more entrepreneurial Chinese minority. During the 1960s and 1970s, industrial development - mainly in export industries, such as in electrical and electronic components - was concentrated in the northern and central regions of the Malaysian peninsular. This export-orientated industry was dependent on foreign direct investments, particularly from Singapore, Japan and the US.

The first half of the 1980s was characterised by the introduction of an industrial policy aimed at broadening the manufacturing sector, as well as promoting the development of heavy industries. In the mid-1980s, the combination of budget deficit and low commodity prices resulted in recession. The economy began to recover in 1987, and the strong economic growth was due largely to foreign direct investments that came about as a consequence of liberalisation policies. The Malaysian economy was deregulated, mainly by the introduction of the *Promotion of Investments Act* of 1986, which allowed foreign investors to obtain 100% of the equity of a Malaysian company, subject to certain limitations. Moreover, state intervention in the economy was reduced (Lim and Nesadurai, 1997, p. 187). Also in 1986, the *National Science and Technology Policy* was introduced with the aim of promoting innovation. The major sectors performing well at that time were those of well-established low-technology manufacturing, such as transport equipment, chemicals, and fabricated metals. The less well-established low-tech textile industry also began to record strong output increases, as did the high- and medium-technology industries, such as electronics and electrical goods. Indeed, by 1987, Malaysia had become one of the world's largest exporters of semiconductors, after Japan and the United States (Sieh and Yew, 1997, p. 132). It was the *First Industrial Master Plan* (IMP) of 1985-1995 that embedded the industrialisation of Malaysia. This resulted in a strong demand for labour in labour-intensive assembly industries, particularly textiles, electronics and electrical consumer products, causing infrastructure bottlenecks. There were labour shortages, in particular for skilled, technical and professional workers.

In 1991, Malaysia introduced both the *National Development Plan*, in which the government dropped all limitations on *Bumiputra* participation, and the *Second Outline Perspective*. Development of infrastructure, the creation of free-trade zones and industrial parks, and the upgrading of ports and airports - necessary prerequisites in attracting foreign and domestic investment - were encouraged not only through deregulation but also the expansion of trade. Notwithstanding the flexibility of immigration restrictions on foreign workers, the most recent policies have been focused on improving education and retraining the workforce. An *Integrated Action Plan* for human resources has been developed, in conjunction with the adoption of a liberal policy on the recruitment of foreign skilled labour. Consequently, from 1987 to mid-1997, the Malaysian economy experienced ten years of uninterrupted high growth and established itself as a major industrial export economy.

However, Malaysia has been lagging behind Singapore in technological development. For instance, total expenditure for 1987-97 on R&D was only 0.24% of the Gross National Product (GNP), and there are only 93 scientists and engineers in R&D per million inhabitants, compared to Singapore's 1.13% and 2,318 (World Bank, 2001). In addition, Malaysia has only 59 personal computers per 1,000 inhabitants, compared with Singapore's 458 (World Bank, 2000). This does not mean that the Malaysian government has been slow to adopt policies promoting technological development. However, its policies have been the result of a simplistic linear view of innovation based on formal research and development activities, as was the case in Europe in the 1960s and 70s. There are two public development agencies concerned with innovation - the *Malaysian Technology Development Corporation* (MTDC) and the *Malaysian Industrial Development Authority* (MIDA) - and two public R&D institutions that lead technological development - the *Standards and Industrial Research Institute of Malaysia* (SIRIM) and the *Malaysian Institute of Microelectronics* (MIMOS) - all of which provide technical assistance to industry[10]. Two more initiatives, the *Vendor Development Programme* and the *Subcontract Exchange Scheme*, have been designed to stimulate the technological capability of the private sectors, particularly by creating linkages between domestic SMEs, large local corporations and TNCs. More recently, the Malaysian government, in recognising the strategic importance of SMEs in the economy, has introduced a whole range of financial incentives and programmes directed at enhancing their competitiveness, particularly in the areas of technological development, information technology, and quality and productivity. These include the following SME-specific programmes[11]:

* *The Industrial Linkage Programme (ILP)*
* *The Technology Development Programme*
* *The Enterprise Development*
* *The Infrastructure Development*
* *The Skills Upgrading Programme*
* *Outreach Programmes*

Many of these programmes are managed by Malaysia's *Small and Medium Industries Development Corporation* (SMIDEC), which was established in 1996 for promoting the development of SMEs in Malaysia.

However, the Malaysian economy is still dependent mostly on manufactured exports produced by foreign-owned subsidiaries, which are mainly assembling plants of imported components. Notwithstanding the fact that Malaysia is now the world's fourth largest semiconductor manufacturer, the value-added is extremely low, as production is based in labour-intensive assembling operations.

Given the rivalry that exists between Malaysia and Singapore, it is not surprising that the Malaysian government, emulating its neighbour, has set ambitious goals for technological development. Malaysia's *Vision 2020*, which includes the *Multimedia Super Corridor* project, promotes the country's industrial development with a view to joining the ranks of developed countries by the year 2020 (Chin, 2000, pp. 1045-8). However, Malaysia still has rather limited expertise in high technology, and much of this technology is controlled by TNCs. Moreover, its indigenous firms have been rather inward-looking, mostly orientated to domestic rather than external trade. The majority of its family-controlled companies have not established links with external networks. Nevertheless, a small number of Malaysian companies in the resource-based industries have established a niche in the international market (Lim and Nesadurai, 1997, p. 212).

Malaysia's deep recession in 1997-8 continued in the first half of 1999, although the economy started to grow again in the year 2000. However, the slow down of the American economy in 2001-02 might reverse the current trend. Seen in general terms, the dependency of the economy on foreign markets and capital is extremely high. In 1998, the economic crisis led the government to require the Bank Negara Malaysia (the central bank) to impose capital and currency controls, in order to restore stability to the economy. The following year, the government eased this controversial regulation, although the imposition of a withdrawal tax has created a disincentive to invest in Malaysia's markets. In March 2001, the Prime Minister, Dr Mahathir, announced a relaxation of the regulations on foreign equity ownership, and is planning to facilitate the purchase of property and other assets by foreigners. Despite all these changes, however, Malaysia has not moved forward to the same extent as Singapore in relation to the liberalisation of its financial market.

2.3.3. The State of Johor: the Southern Gateway to Malaysia

The Malaysian State of Johor, with a population with 2.5 million, is the third largest in the country (19,984 sq km) and is situated at the southern extremity of the Malay Peninsula, across the strait from Singapore. Up to 1985, the economy of Johor was based mainly on agriculture, and lagged behind the northern and central regions of the country. However, manufacturing growth soon accelerated, and Johor joined Singapore and the Province of Riau (Indonesia) to form a growth triangle, as a consequence of the wider regionalisation process taking place in South-East Asia. The shift from the primary to the secondary sector in Johor follows the national pattern of economic transformation. For instance, the creation of a number of mainly low-tech industrial estates in Johor, and an export-processing zone at Pasir Gudang, has been a success, resulting in the establishment of a number of specialised high-technology industrial parks. Economically, Johor is now one of the most advanced states of the Malaysian federation. It is the third most industrialised state, accounting for 10% of the country's GDP[12].

The State Government of Johor has given high priority to the development of manufacturing through its principal development agency, the Johor Corporation. During the last fifteen years, the state has encouraged inward investment with various tax incentives. Foreign direct investment in manufacturing in Johor has come from TNCs, and their subsidiaries already based in Johor, as well as from Singaporean companies, some of which have either relocated in Johor or transferred production activities to the state (Grunsven et al., 1995a, p. 21). The major investors in Johor are primarily from Singapore, followed by Japan and Taiwan (Table 2.1). Investment in manufacturing has traditionally been concentrated in the following sectors: textiles and

Table 2.1: Johor: Approved Projects by Country of Origin (1993-1997)

COUNTRY	FOREIGN INVESTMENT (RM millions)				
	1993	1994	1995	1996	1997
Singapore	241	481	530	3,236	809
Taiwan	8	129	250	181	1,090
Japan	169	399	516	601	157
Hong Kong	5	84	128	2	N/A
United States	39	48	165	157	610
Australia	-	4	52	3	N/A
United Kingdom	5	5	126	8	N/A
France	5	50	97	-	N/A
Others	87	101	516	524	37
Total	559	1,245	2,379	4,712	2,703*

* Provisional figure; N/A: figures not available.
Source: MIDA

footwear, engineering, machinery, electrical consumer goods and electronics, and petro-chemicals. Foreign direct investment (FDI) involves not only transfer of capital but more importantly transfer of technology. However, it is unlikely that such investment can provide sufficient technology improvements to sustain high growth without developing an indigenous technological capacity.

In the early 1990s, the State of Johor had ambitious plans to develop its capital, Johor Bahru, into a 'major growth pole and modern technopolis' by the year 2005 (Abdullah, 1996, p. 197). However, the existing industrial base in Johor at that time was weak, and the inter-linkages of local SMEs and TNCs were non-existent (Grunsven et al., 1995b, p. 7). Moreover, due to insufficient know-how, local SMEs have so far been unable to produce high-technology products. Therefore, in order to achieve its goal, the state needs to promote joint ventures between foreign and locally owned firms, thereby facilitating the transfer of technology and the process of learning. Some such transfer and learning has started to take place in the wider spatial context of the SIJORI growth triangle.

Undoubtedly, the industrial development of Johor has been associated with the restructuring of the economy of Singapore, as the largest part of Singaporean investment in Malaysia flows to its neighbour. This points to the regionalisation of industrial production and economic activity in general, encompassing not only economic but also political and social links. Grunsven et al. (1995b, p. 73), in their thorough survey of the industrial structure of Johor, found that the local electronic industry was strongly integrated with that of Singapore. They also realised that face-to-face contacts assisted by geographical proximity were important for procuring inputs from Johor (Grunsven et al., 1995b, pp. 86-87). These findings are supported by the current study.

2.3.4 The Singapore-Johor Cross-Border Agglomeration and the Logic of Spillover

The role of Singapore as a regional hub in South-East Asia has been reinforced by its regionalisation strategy, especially since the establishment of growth triangles and industrial parks. The term *growth triangle* is synonymous with that of the innovative milieu. It is attributed to the present Prime Minister of Singapore, Goh Chok Tong, who, as Deputy Prime Minister in 1989, used it to describe the trilateral co-operation taking place between Singapore, the southern-most part of the Malaysian State of Johor, and the nearby Indonesian islands of Bintan and Batam, part of Riau Province (hence the acronym SIJORI). The term has since been used to describe the rapid development and economic co-operation of a number of geographically adjacent studied by researchers (Than and Tang, 1996; Lim, 1996; Debrah et al., 2000).

The SIJORI growth triangle is thus a partnership arrangement between three ASEAN member states. The strategy is to combine the capital, infrastructure and expertise of Singapore with the natural and labour resources of Johor and Riau. In practice, Singapore plays a leading role in the triangle, given the fact that direct links between Johor and the province of Riau are still very weak[13].

There are two related factors that have contributed to the development of the SIJORI growth triangle. The first of these is the regionalisation strategy of TNCs, which tend to agglomerate their offshore production in a few selected localities rather than disperse their value-added chain activities in a wider geographical area. In the early 1990s, Ng and Wong observed that competition for attracting inward investment from TNCs was taking place among regional agglomerations rather than individual countries (1991). This resulted in the emergence of large regional urban poles, such as Singapore and, to a lesser extent, Bangkok and Hong Kong. The second factor, according to Ng and Wong, is the emergence of large indigenous companies which grow in size, spilling over into neighbouring regions. For instance, companies such as the Malaysia Mining Corporation, UMW Corporation, and Sime Darby Bhd. in Malaysia, and the Keppel Corporation, Singapore Technology Group, and Overseas-Chinese Banking Corporation in Singapore, were increasingly forming strategic alliances and joint ventures in neighbouring areas as part of their internationalisation strategy (Ng and Wong, 1991; Yeung, 1998; Yeoh and Chang, 2001).

A study in the early 1990s on the impact of TNCs' investments in Malaysia, Singapore and Thailand revealed that the majority of TNCs based in Singapore were selecting Johor as the base for their expansion into Malaysia (Natarajan and Tan, 1992, pp. 18-19). Their main reason for choosing Johor was its geographical proximity to Singapore. The same study also found that linkages between firms' operations in Johor and Singapore were strong. Grunsven et al. (1995a, p. 54), in their survey on locational factors, pointed out that infrastructure facilities that allow face-to-face contact with firms in Singapore was the most important consideration, rather than different factor endowment. The geographical proximity was also important, as shown by Grunsven et al. (1995a, p. 62). The same researchers also found (1995b) that there was a high level of labour mobility in the developed industrial estates in Johor, implying diffusion of technology and learning.

In the late 1980s, the Singapore government assisted in the development of industrial parks in Johor. At the same time, Johor sought further technical assistance from its neighbour in order to set up a skills development centre, as well as a science and technology park (Ng and Wong, 1991). However, despite these early signs of collaboration, the Singapore-Johor side of the growth triangle - in comparison to the Singapore-Riau side - has not been formalised, and no bilateral agreement has taken place. It is alleged that the Malaysian central government has not been forthcoming, until quite recently, in supporting the participation of Johor in the triangle (Chia, 1996, p. 178). The unequal Federal-State relationship sometimes hampers the growth of businesses, particularly in matters relating to land development, and this increases the transaction costs of doing business in Johor. On the other hand, spatial development in Singapore is driven by central government only, and the city-state has therefore been more effective in co-ordinating economic and spatial policies[14].

Johor and Singapore have strong historical affinities tracing back to the post-colonial era, and, as mentioned earlier, strong business links. However, since the separation of Singapore from the Malayan Federation in 1965, relations between the two neighbouring countries have been volatile. In 1997, comments by the Senior

Minister of Singapore, Lee Kuan Yew, on the backwardness of Johor, caused a diplomatic rift. Da Cunha, referring to an 'unequal dependence', points out that Singapore is far more dependent on Malaysia than vice versa, not only because the latter is larger in size and population, but also because its water supplies and air space are vital to Singapore's existence (Da Cunha, 1998, p. 64).

However, Singapore has consistently been one of the main investors in Malaysia, especially in Johor, as shown in Table 2.1. A survey in 1992 by the Singapore Manufacturers' Association revealed that approximately 20% of its respondents had invested in Johor. The majority of them were larger companies - only 39% were SMEs - and were operating in the electrical goods and electronics industry. The major reason for investing in Johor was labour availability and proximity to Singapore, although, ironically, shortage of labour eventually became a problem in Johor, as did delays caused by immigration checks and slow customs clearance (SMA, 1992, pp. 1-5). Many of our sample companies on both sides of the Johor Strait said that customs and immigration delays are still a problem, notwithstanding the fact that Johor has recently been physically connected to Singapore by a second bridge, making daily commuting easier. Tourism and shopping spillovers from Singapore to Johor have also increased significantly, and have led to a large increase in investment in commercial property and in the leisure sector.

The economies of Johor and Singapore are interdependent. Johor can offer land and labour at a lower cost than its neighbour, while Singapore can offer managerial and professional expertise lacking across the strait. From Johor's point of view, the state capital of Johor Bahru has benefited immensely from the economic spillover due to its geographical proximity to Singapore (Debrah et al., 2000, p. 317). The latter functions as a regional centre for South-East Asia, offering a variety of services including worldwide air and maritime transport connections which are of great value to Johor. Nevertheless, Johor itself has a relatively developed infrastructure, including an export-processing free zone and two expanding ports which are beginning to challenge its neighbour's monopoly. One of the advantages of this infrastructure endowment has been that semi-finished products can be transported from Singapore to Johor and fully assembled, tested and packaged, then shipped back to Singapore for worldwide exportation. The strengthening of synergies between Singapore and Johor is but a modest contribution to the economic integration of Singapore and Malaysia. It is nevertheless the best example of cross-border co-operation within ASEAN, given the fact that the grand scheme of ASEAN economic integration has so far failed to materialise, since it is not yet politically ready to emulate the single-market concept of the EU.

Naturally, regional integration depends on the extent of economic complementarities. Such complementarities, as shown in Table 2.2, are exceptionally high in the Singapore-Johor agglomeration.

The exploitation of complementarities is taking place, and Johor has become the site to which labour- and land-intensive manufacturing has been moved by both TNCs and Singaporean firms. However, this relocation has not reduced the extent of firms' operations in Singapore, and the majority continue to maintain and even upgrade their

Table 2.2: Salient Issues in Complementarities between Singapore and Johor

Labour Recruitment and Skills	Singapore has a low unemployment rate and is facing labour shortages, especially of manual and clerical workers
	Johor has a relatively large unskilled labour supply, helped by the influx of migrant workers from neighbouring Malaysian states
Land	Singapore land is very scarce and expensive
	Johor land is relatively available and land prices are much lower
Natural resources	Singapore has hardly any of the natural resources (including water) necessary for the operation of natural resource-intensive industries
	Johor has abundant natural resources
Communication, distribution, and business support systems	Singapore is an important entrepot (i.e. a port that has developed as a commercial hub, with related industries) and has a sophisticated transport and communications infrastructure
	Johor benefits from the proximity of Singapore's facilities
Quality of life and recreational activities	Singapore has many cultural and urban facilities
	Johor has an attractive recreational environment

Source: Adapted from Ng and Wong, 1991, and Debrah et al., 2000.

operations there. Furthermore, relocation increases the comparative advantage of the agglomeration over other likely competitors. Technology spillovers from the R&D institutions and activities of TNCs - most of which have their research facilities in Singapore - are also taking place, together with economies of scales in learning. Business networks across the Strait, based on family ties, are also important mechanisms by which many SMEs interact, learn and eventually innovate.

As noted above, the Singapore-Johor cross-border area is becoming an important agglomeration for high-technology industries. For example, the electrical goods and electronics industry is growing fast, and evolving from low-tech products and assembly manufacturing into a sophisticated, high-tech, capital-intensive industry. The participation of many regional firms in supply chains, and the continuous flow of components, intermediary goods and services within the agglomeration, all positively influence the integration of the region. Furthermore, these interactions permit economies of scale in learning to take place. However, learning behaviour patterns differ between the SMEs and TNCs that dominate the regional agglomeration. SMEs, being too small and inexperienced, cannot afford to participate in international networks and are more likely to establish network activities within the regional/local economy; TNCs, by contrast, do have access to international networks.

The advent during the second half of 1997 of the so-called Asian crisis had a detrimental effect on the development of the Singapore-Johor agglomeration. The immediate consequence was the devaluation of currencies, particularly the Malaysian Ringgit, and a drop in stock market values. As a result, there was a build-up of overcapacity in many sectors across the Strait, from empty office blocks and shopping malls to idle factories. Singapore suffered less from the financial and currency crisis than its neighbour. Nevertheless, Singaporean investors in Malaysia saw their investments suffer from falling asset values, corporate debts, shrinking demand and cash flow problems.

The financial crisis of 1997-98 was handled differently by the two countries. The Singapore government introduced a variety of measures to help local firms, such as reducing rentals, wages, and other businesses costs (Chia, 1999, pp. 64-65). More importantly, it launched a reform agenda for further liberalisation and restructuring, including that of its banking sector. By contrast, Malaysia imposed exchange controls and a fixed rate with the US dollar. This was perceived to be a high-risk strategy, given the fact that Malaysia is in fact an open, export-led economy (Athukorala, 1999, p. 37). However, the industrial success of both countries depends on a small number of sectors, such as electronics, and this has led to over-reliance on exports to the United States. International trade and open markets are considered to be vital for the growth of the economies of both Singapore and Malaysia, as well as the rest of the ASEAN member states. The financial crisis did not change this, but it raised questions about the region's dependence on global trading.

2.4 EU-ASEAN Technological Co-operation

In the post-war era, many European countries - for a variety of reasons (including the constant strain on East-West relations, and the independence of former colonies) - lost interest in Asia in general and in South-East Asia in particular. Furthermore, latent animosity persists towards former colonial powers within many Asian countries. Despite this, economic co-operation began to develop between Europe and ASEAN during the early 1970s. In 1972, ASEAN established trade links with the EU that culminated eight years later in a Co-operation Agreement, signed in March 1980 at the second ASEAN-EC Ministerial Meeting (AEMM) held in Kuala Lumpur[15]. This agreement - which is still the only legal framework that governs relations between the two trading groups - set out the structure for institutionalised meetings, and closer economic and commercial co-operation. It was undertaken in order to reduce ASEAN's trade dependency on the US and Japan, and offered a framework of political, economic and technological consultation. Ministerial meetings between the two regions are still taking place annually, and topics discussed have included industrial co-operation, science and technology, and research and development.

The first EU-ASEAN Economic Ministers' meeting took place in Bangkok in 1985. The outcome was an Economic Agreement aimed at expanding trade between the two regional blocs. ASEAN countries hoped to improve production through technology transfer, and to attract more EU firms to locate in the region, while the EU hoped to encourage SMEs to invest in ASEAN, which they facilitated by supporting meetings on industrial collaboration and technology transfer, as well as assisting in research (Yeung et al., 1999, p. 81).

The rather broad EC-ASEAN Co-operation Agreement was soon followed by bilateral agreements between the member countries of the two blocs. As the EU and ASEAN have expanded, their new member countries (with the exception of Myanmar) have gradually acceded to the Co-operation Agreement.[16] However, the Agreement - which focused primarily on trade - was seen as a 'product of its time', since the main instrument for carrying out policy agreements was that of developmental aid and co-operation (Forster, 1999: 745) rather than trade and investment. Moreover, the Agreement's good intentions did not bear fruit, and relations between ASEAN and the EU remained 'virtually non-existent' (Yeung et al., 1999, p. 81).

By the early 1990s, it was clear that there had been no major steps towards closer economic co-operation between the two trading groups. The EU was preoccupied with the completion of its Single European Market and was frustrated by the fact that ASEAN integration was not progressing (Hine, 2000, p. 14) and ASEAN itself was focusing on its contradictory enlargement plans concerned with the incorporation of Vietnam and Myanmar into the Association.

However, the transformation of the European Community into a European Union, brought about by the Maastricht Treaty in 1993, led to the need for a revaluation of the EU-ASEAN relationship. Co-operation intensified in 1994, during the 11th AEMM in Karlsruhe, Germany. An important outcome of this meeting was agreement on the creation of an Eminent Persons Group (EPG) for developing a new approach to EU-ASEAN political, economic and cultural relations fit for the 21st century. The proposed priorities in the co-operation have now shifted from trade to a series of discrete activities aimed at the alleviation of poverty, development of human resources, improvement in health and family planning, increase in women's participation in economic life, respect for human rights and the protection of the environment.

The justification for this new era of co-operation is found in the European Commission's Communication document of 1994 entitled *'Towards a New Asia Strategy'*.[17] The explicit intent of the Communication, which was endorsed by the European Parliament in 1995, was the 'strengthening of the EU's political and economic presence' in the wider Asian region. This included Vietnam, Laos, Myanmar and Cambodia (all prospective members of ASEAN), but also China, India, Pakistan, Bangladesh, Sri Lanka and South Korea.

In the late 1980s and the 1990s, trade improved dramatically, with an increase in manufactured goods exported from ASEAN to the EU. Germany was one of the main destinations for exports, followed by the UK, France, Italy and the Netherlands. The EU member states, for their part, also became a major exporter to ASEAN, mainly in transportation equipment, electrical equipment and electronics. The EU accounts for about 20 per cent of foreign direct investment in the ASEAN countries (Tan, 1996, p. 188), the majority going to Singapore and Malaysia, which together attract approximately 65 per cent. However, the recurrent economic crises and the increasing competition in technology-related FDI from China have decreased the inflows of FDI to South-East Asia (UNCTAD, 2001, p. 4). Although the European Union is one of the leading investors in ASEAN, the countries of the Association have minimal investments in the European Union. Nevertheless, they are encouraging their companies to invest in Europe, and this is especially true of Singapore and Malaysia. One example is Malaysia's involvement in the West of England[18], where the port of Bristol is the main point of entry for Proton cars.

The first Asia-Europe summit meeting (ASEM), which was initiated by the Prime Minister of Singapore and took place in Bangkok in 1996, was a belated commencement of closer relationships with Europe. At the summit, the then seven member countries of ASEAN, along with China, Japan and South Korea, met with the fifteen member countries of the EU. It is clear that, for both sides, the motivation behind the promotion of closer relationships was economic co-operation. The Asian countries challenged the EU to reduce tariffs in the same way that the Asia Pacific Economic Co-operation (APEC), an alternative trade grouping, has done. Asian members wanted increased access to the EU market, more European investment, and the establishment of dialogue. It was also agreed that an annual meeting of Asian and European economic ministers would take place. The EU has been increasing its presence in technologically intensive industries, R&D, and scientific co-operation. Indeed, foreign direct investment has grown dramatically, with Germany again the largest foreign investor, followed by the Netherlands and the UK. At that time, these three countries accounted for 80 per cent of EU foreign investment in ASEAN (Yeung et al., 1999, p. 97). The importance of creating close links was also stressed at the second ASEM summit in London in 1998, as well as the third, in Seoul in the year 2000. Although ASEM is informal and does not have a permanent organisational entity, it has nevertheless established two important institutions, the Asia-Europe Foundation and the Asia-Europe Environment and Technology Centre; it also created the ASEM Trust Fund in order to provide assistance to Asian countries affected by the 1997-8 financial crisis.

According to Ljungkvist, inter-industry trade, which used to dominate EU-ASEAN trade, is now very much in decline. Intra-industry trade, on the other hand, is growing fast, as predicted by the traditional trade theory (Ljungkvist, 1998, p. 97), and this could lead to large dynamic gains by increasing incentives to innovate. New exports to the EU consist of textiles, machinery and, in particular, electronics. However, the comparative advantage of the ASEAN region in exporting machinery and electronics is as great as the trade statistics suggest, because many of these products still have a high content of imported components (Ljungkvist, 1998, p. 97). In addition, free trade between the two blocs is hampered by the European Union's multi-layered network of associations and preferential agreements. This point was raised by the Malaysian subsidiary of an American company during the author's fieldwork visit, who argued that the company was treated unfairly by the EU, since it had to satisfy the requirement that its exported machinery should be built using at least the minimum proportion of European components. The new *General System of Preferences* is also deemed to be a disadvantage to the ASEAN countries, because when a country becomes a successful exporter, it eventually has to leave the system and no more preferential treatment is given. As a consequence of this, one Japanese subsidiary in Malaysia is considering relocation in Indonesia, in which the preference system is still applicable. The European Union's Common Agricultural Policy is also a barrier to the export of some agricultural produce from the ASEAN countries. Furthermore, the use of anti-dumping action against some exports, particularly consumer electronics, and voluntary export restrictions, or even the inclusion of non-trade issues into the World Trade Organisation (WTO) agreements, have made some observers question the participation of the European Union in the WTO as an equal economic partner (Sieh, 1997, pp. 150-151).

In 2001, the European Commission updated its 1994 Communication with a new version entitled *'Europe and Asia: A Strategic Framework for Enhanced Partnerships'*.[19] In this Communication, the Commission reiterates the economic and political importance of Asia to Europe, noting that it is aware of the political impact of the financial crisis, and therefore aspiring to increase its dialogue with the region. More importantly, the new Communication takes a rather holistic view of EU-Asian collaboration, and signals its readiness for an ever-closer relationship with Asia. It acknowledges 'the need for reinforced inter-regional scientific and technological co-operation to foster common analysis of and solutions to shared regional and global problems' (p.19). In relation to ASEAN, the Commission expresses the wish to enhance co-operation between the two regions, particularly in new-technology sectors.

While this section has focused briefly on the evolution of wider collaborative relations between Europe and South-East Asia, it has nevertheless shown that interest in inter-regional co-operation has fluctuated considerably over time, according to circumstances. Predictably, such fluctuations reflect not only the different agendas pursued by the EU and ASEAN (Palmujoki, 1997), but also the fact that ASEAN itself has not yet developed a comprehensible strategy for Europe. The consensus is that EU-ASEAN relations are 'asymmetric', because the EU has been more important to ASEAN countries than vice versa (Slater, 2000, p. 238).

Notes

[1] The works of Hägerstrand on innovation diffusion, and François Perroux on growth pole theory, highlight the importance of locational factors for innovation. Other authors have also emphasised the locational dimension and regional applicability of the product cycle, and the filter down approaches (Sternberg, 1996a, pp. 519-521). Miozzo and Montobbio (2000) reassess the product cycle model in the light of the evolution of knowledge-based economy and interactive learning on the innovative performance of regions (pp. 114-130). For a theoretical framework that explains interactive learning between firms and external actors, see Meeus et al., (2001).

[2] The difficulties in establishing a definition of the region and its effect on EU policy have been discussed by Drèze (1993).

[3] The South West of England consists of the counties and unitary authorities of Gloucestershire, South

Gloucestershire, Swindon and Wiltshire, Bristol, Somerset, Bath & North East Somerset, North Somerset, Bournemouth, Dorset and Poole, Devon, Torbay and Plymouth, and Cornwall and the Isles of Scilly.

[4] Sir Michael Lickiss, Chairman of the Regional Development Agency for the South West, cf. Braddon and Konstadakopulos (1999, p. 10).

[5] 'Malaysia deal *"won through threat"* ', *Financial Times*, 26 July 2000

[6] *The Economist*, A Survey of South-East Asia, 12 February 2000.

[7] 'S. Korean police seal off ASEM site to avoid clashes', *The Straits Times*, 20 October 2000.

[8] The innovative performance of local firms has up to now been mediocre. Incentives such as Research Development Assistance Schemes and the Research Incentive Scheme for Companies were made available for both local and foreign firms.

[9] Schemes such as the Local Industry Upgrading Programme and the Promising Local Enterprises Programme are focusing on SMEs - many of which are suppliers to TNCs - for upgrading their productivity and improving their managerial capability.

[10] Malaysia has a total of 33 public sector R&D institutions and 8 universities. Some of these institutions conduct a wide range of R&D activities, while others are more specific. (Lecture presented by Mr. Anuar Md. Nor, at the WIFO-IFIA International Symposium on the Commercialisation of Patented Inventions, Kuala Lumpur, August 1996.)

[11] Ministry of International Trade and Industry, (2002), *'Malaysia, Policy, Incentives and Facilities for SMEs'*, Kuala Lumpur: MITI.

http://www.smidec.gov.my/homepage/homepage12.nsf/a1598a5be7b1ebaa4825696f0031bfef/2ae9e2055f69f7bc48256ca7000ffb88/$FILE/publish.pdf, accessed 18/2/2003.

[12] State of Johor Statistics at http://www.johordt.gov.my/page1.php?screen=bab3_1.htm, accessed 18/2/2003.

[13] There are a number of other regional co-operation initiatives in the ASEAN region that have been described as growth triangles. These are: the Greater Mekong Sub-regional Co-operation Scheme, the Indonesia-Malaysia-Thailand Growth Area, and the Brunei-Indonesia-Malaysia-Philippines East ASEAN Growth Area (Than, 1996, pp.1-2). The rationale for the creation of growth triangles is both the large inflow of foreign investment and the desire to exploit economies of scales and vertical integration in production. The driving force in such development is the business sector, but governments can act as facilitators by removing border barriers and offering financial inducements.

[14] This point was raised by an anonymous referee.

[15] European Council Regulation (EEC) No. 1440/80 of 30 May 1980 concerning the conclusion of the *Cooperation Agreement* between the European Economic Community and Indonesia, Malaysia, the Philippines, Singapore and Thailand, all members countries of ASEAN.

[16] However, given the intergovernmental status of ASEAN, its new member states could accede to the Cooperation Agreement through the signing of special protocols. Initially, the Agreement included only the five original members of ASEAN (i.e. Thailand, Malaysia, Indonesia, the Philippines and Singapore), but then the new member nations, Brunei, Vietnam, Laos and Cambodia signed these special protocols. Burma/Myanmar, however, remains outside the Agreement, due to concern over violations of human rights and the country's lack of progress towards democracy. Within the EU, new member states automatically become members of the Agreement.

[17] Commission of European Communities, *Towards a New Asia Strategy*, COM(94) 314 final, Brussels 13.07.1994.

[18] For instance, in 2002 the Malaysian energy group YTL Power bought Wessex Water, the utility company based in Bristol, from the bankrupt energy trader Enron.

[19] COM(2001) 469 final.

Part II: The Empirical Comparative Analysis

Chapter 3:

Innovation in the West of England

This chapter presents the qualitative results of the empirical investigation carried out in the West of England sub-regional cluster, namely the triangle formed by the Bristol-Bath, Gloucester-Cheltenham and Swindon/M4 corridor areas. These constitute not only the principal agglomeration of high-technology companies found in the South West of England region, but also one of the most important in Europe. The fieldwork was carried out in the above three urban centres, using the local postcode areas to define the catchment area for firms viable for study. This area has a critical mass of spatially concentrated high-technology firms, and educational and research institutions.

The objective of the empirical study was to investigate whether and how SMEs interact with each other, as well as with other economic actors in the West of England, thereby identifying the learning processes described in Chapter 1, deriving from the innovative milieu or cluster model of analysis. A further aim was to establish whether co-operative modes of interaction, and external economies such as that of collective learning, exist in the West of England. In addition, the survey investigated the existence, form, intensiveness and quality of firms' linkages and the motivation behind them. A further task was the identification and evaluation of the effectiveness of the most important regional 'collective' actors concerned, and the way they are involved in a formal or informal way in facilitating collective and collaborative learning processes.

The chapter is organised as follows: first, a profile of regional high-technology SMEs is constructed, including the firms' size, growth rate, innovative activity, number of breakthrough innovations, and their sources of know-how and knowledge. Second, the results of the survey are presented with regard to the firms' relationships and linkages with suppliers, subcontractors and customers. Third, the effect of regional specific advantages necessary for firms' development is analysed. Finally, the regional channels of knowledge acquisition are identified.

Two further chapters conclude this section. Chapter 4 contains an analysis of the survey results obtained from the Singapore-Johor agglomeration. Chapter 5 compares the two agglomerations, and discusses the discrepancies identified between the empirical analyses and the innovative milieu model.

3.1 The Profile of Innovative Regional Firms

The empirical investigation was based on interviews with the managers of more than sixty SMEs, using a standardised questionnaire. Further information and data came from an in-depth network analysis case study (some of the results of which were shown in Figure 1.1), as well as a number of open interviews with regional decision-makers, and round-table discussions. The sample of randomly selected firms is drawn from industrial sectors which are technologically intensive and have the ability to grow rapidly. It consists of SMEs that are not only involved in high-technology manufacturing but are also providing services. These latter were included because the service industry is becoming an important contributor to the economy of the South West of England. The selection of high-technology sectors was guided by the definition provided by Butchard (1987), which was also employed by Keeble et al. (1997), with some small modifications. Sampling was designed to include companies of between 5 and 250 employees. However, before interpreting the results, one limitation of the data needs to be taken into account. Not all regional SMEs are accustomed to answering questions about innovation outputs, labour turnover and exports, so we encouraged them to report approximate 'round' figures (i.e. 5 per cent), which may have introduced some 'noise' to the data.

The structure of the sampled firms, showing size and location, is shown in Table 3.1, while the clustering of innovative SMEs is illustrated in Figure 3.1.

Table 3.1: Size and Location of Sampled Firms used in the 1998-99 Survey in the West of England

Location of Firms	<50 employees	50-100 employees	>100 employees	Total firms
Gloucester-Cheltenham	9	6	6	21
Bristol-Bath	14	3	4	21
Swindon/M4	12	2	5	19
Total (%)	35 (57%)	11 (18%)	15 (25%)	61 (100%)

Source: Own survey.

The vast majority of sampled firms (75%) are small businesses in high-technology sectors, employing less than 100 workers. They are a representative sample of innovative firms in the West of England. However, before embarking on a more detailed picture of the innovative milieu characteristics identified, some general characteristics of the sampled firms must be given:

* The average age of the firms is 16 years, the youngest being one year old and the oldest 62 years old. Only 21% are young firms, established after 1990; more than half (54%) were established between 1970 and 1990, and 25% before 1970.

* Approximately a quarter of the firms belong to the engineering sector, a fifth in electronics and telecommunication, a similar proportion in the computer services (mostly software and training) and one tenth in the medical equipment and instrumentation sector.

* The majority (three quarters) of the firms are regionally owned companies rather than a subsidiary or a part of a group of companies. The Bristol-Bath area has the highest number of indigenous companies, while the Swindon/M4 corridor area has the

lowest. From the interviews with managers of indigenous companies, it was established that some of the businesses were founded by individuals who had some previous experience in a similar line of business, and had their origins in the West of England. A number of other companies were the result of spin-offs from well-known larger national firms such as Racal, Raychem and Thorn-EMI, or from European multinationals such as Linotype-Hell (from which two of our sample companies in the Cheltenham and Gloucester area trace their origin).

The sample represents a considerable part of the regional economy, as the 61 firms employ approximately 4,800 workers and generate a turnover of more than £1.5 billion. The firms were asked to report the percentage of their employees who are designated as either scientists/engineers or administrators/managers. This percentage is an important yardstick in identifying the extent of skilled human resources necessary for the innovative process. The average percentage was 63, irrespective of company size. However, companies involved in electronics and telecommunications manufacturing, and in software services, reported an above average percentage of skilled workforce. At the same time, the location of companies within the agglomeration appears to be significant. There is a higher concentration of skilled workforce in the Swindon/M4 corridor in comparison with the Bristol-Bath and Cheltenham-Gloucester areas.

An indication of how our sample of firms performed during the five years prior to the study is shown in changes in the number of employees and in business turnover, as well as the reported level of profits for 1998. This indicates that the majority of our sampled regional companies were performing well. For instance, 62% of firms reported that they had increased their number of employees, and 81% that they increased their turnover, while 20% and 8% respectively reported static employment growth and static turnover. Finally, only 17% and 11% of firms respectively mentioned a decrease in employment or turnover. The reported profitability levels reinforce this picture. Of the sampled firms, 30% stated that profits for 1998 were 'good' or 'excellent', while 50% said that they were 'reasonable'. Only 20% had made no profits, or recorded a loss.

3.2 Regional Innovators and their Sources of Innovation

The survey suggests that its fifteen externally controlled companies (25% of the total sample) are important for the innovative performance of the region as a whole. Eleven of them stated that they have their own R&D department, of which ten were located in the South West of England. Moreover, five of these externally controlled companies have patented a product or a process innovation during the last five years, while two have produced a *breakthrough*, i.e. a new product or service, such as Dyson's vacuum cleaner (see Table 3.2).

Of the 46 regionally owned companies, representing 75% of the sample, 29 (or 48%) have an R&D department, and of these the majority (40%) are located within the region. In addition, 16 of these companies (or 26%) reported that they had patented a product or a process innovation during the last five years. This brings the total number of companies that patented an innovation to 21, representing 34% of the total sample. Moreover, eight of the regionally owned companies reported breakthrough innovations with an application to semi-manufactured goods or to niche products and/or services. This brings the total number of breakthrough innovations to 10, representing 16% of the firm sample.

Figure 3.1: Clustering of Innovative SMEs in the West of England

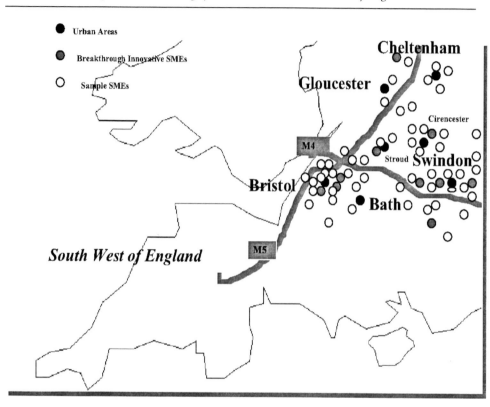

An additional indication of innovative activity in the region is the overall average R&D spending reported for 1998. The average R&D intensity is a respectable 6.3% (well above the OECD estimates for European firms, but below the 10.8% of American companies)[1]. This compares favourably to the figure of 4.7% identified in the author's 1997 survey, which included a larger sample of innovative but also low-technology firms covering the whole of the South West of England and South Wales (Konstadakopulos, 1997). Another way to look at a firm's innovative activity is through information reported by the firm regarding the purchase of different types of advanced equipment or machinery, licensed products, and advanced software during the last three years. The resulting qualitative information allows us to take into account the informal R&D activities of smaller firms, which may be underestimated in the firm's report about patents and breakthrough innovations. The present study revealed that

84% of SMEs purchased advanced equipment, machinery, licensed products or advanced software.

A significant amount of regional firms (67%) sell at least a quarter of their products or services abroad. Export specialisation is generally the result of long-term historical processes, where learning and knowledge acquisition between users and producers of technology is a continuous and significant part of the process. In addition, export demand is very important in generating innovation.

Table 3.2: Innovation Output of Firms in Manufacturing and Services (1993-1998) in Three Urban Agglomerations in the West of England, and Average R&D Intensity in 1998

	Firms with Innovations	Firms with no Innovations	All firms
Number of firms	22	39	61
... in Cheltenham-Gloucester (with breakthrough innovations[1])	8 (3)	13	21 (3)
... in Bristol-Bath (with breakthrough innovations[1])	8 (3)	13	21 (3)
... in Swindon/M4 corridor (with breakthrough innovations[1])	6 (4)	13	19 (4)
Average R&D spending in 1998 as % of sales[2]	8.7%	5.0%	6.3%

Total 61 firms
Source: Own survey.
[1] These include design and manufacturing of specialist engineering (3), innovations in satellite software and communication systems (2), magnetic material scanning systems (1), semiconductors for mobile phones (1), software systems (1), medical instruments (1), and plastic materials for electronics (1).
[2] Arithmetic average.

Companies' managers were asked to report the main sources of know-how - e.g. their R&D department, their staff, other companies, government departments, or universities (Figure 3.2) - leading to their most important innovations. It appears that internal sources are more important for innovation than external ones (Table 3.3). The most significant source seems to be the firm's staff, followed by R&D or design departments. However, external sources are also important, in particular other companies, including customers, suppliers, subcontractors and competitors. These are crucial to the process of co-operation, and are examined in detail later.

Table 3.3: Principal Input of Learning for the Most Important Innovations for Firms in the West of England

Learning input	Times mentioned	
Internal source: firm's R&D and/or design departments	33	
firm's staff	47	
Total		**80**
External source: other company(ies)	16	
government department	4	
university	13	
other (associations, Web sites, etc.)	7	
Total		**40**

Total 61 firms
Note: More than one answer allowed.
Source: Own survey.

Figure 3.2: Sources of Learning in the West of England

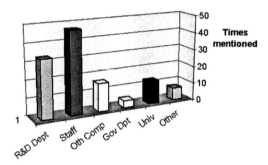

3.3 Regional Collaboration in Product and Process Development

In our previous discussion on the theoretical conceptualisation of the innovative milieu, we noted that learning requires high levels of interaction and exchanges of technological information, as well as collaboration in product development between firms and institutions in the regional agglomeration. Our sample companies were therefore asked to report whether they had a partner collaborating in the development of one of their latest products or processes. Figure 3.3 reveals that the companies' customers and suppliers/subcontractors are usually the main collaborating partners, followed by a university department, or other unspecified partners and consultants. However, when managers were asked whether or not it was important for the future earnings of their company that no other party gain access to the knowledge behind the development of their new products or services, exactly three quarters of them stated that this was the case. This suggests a rather individualistic and non-collaborative disposition on the part of these managers.

Figure 3.3: Collaboration in Product/Process Development in the West of England

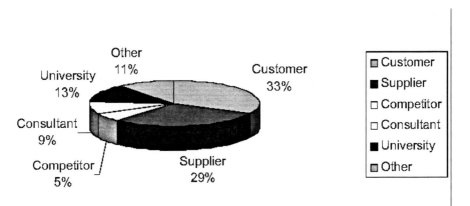

3.4 Inter-firm Linkages, Networks and Collaboration

The theoretical review provided earlier indicated that informal linkages, the socialisation of firms' managers and regional interdependencies are very significant factors in the clustering of innovative firms. Therefore, our priority is to understand how innovative firms in the three agglomerations interact with each other, and what type of relations, linkages and networks exist between companies and regional institutions which may contribute to the creation of a regional collective learning capability. For instance, in northern Italy, the well-developed system of suppliers and subcontractors working together in particular sectors is one of the main assets of local companies. At the same time, relationships with customers are also important, particularly for the creation of new products and services. Meeus et al., drawing from their work in a Dutch region, indicate that interactive learning between innovator firms and their suppliers is associated with the quality of the resource base (percentage of higher-educated employees) and the complexity and structuring of innovative activity (2001, p. 426). Mitra's conceptual paper on the importance of 'making connections' argues that innovation is the result of interaction between various organisations, technologies and people. Learning derived from such interaction is therefore the basis of the firm's innovative activity (Mitra, 2000).

The survey results, which shed some light on inter-firm linkages, networks and forms of collaboration, are presented in Tables 3.4 to 3.9. A total of 79% of the sampled firms' managers stated that they believe that meeting and discussing business with their suppliers/subcontractors is important for their company. Frequent contact with suppliers was reported by 42% of firms, while 44% have occasional contact, and the remaining 14% no contact at all. The most common type of linkage with other regional firms is based on informal relationships. These relationships normally come about through social occasions (mentioned 10 times), or meetings and seminars organised by local associations or organisations (mentioned 8 times). Such informal meetings take place in a wide range of networking arrangements, such as Business Link breakfast meetings, Department of Trade and Industry dinners and lunches, Engineering Employers Federation meetings, Society of Motor Manufactures and Traders events, Motor Shows and Trade Fairs.

Spatial proximity also plays an important role for companies (mentioned 7 times). In regional clusters, firms co-operate but also compete. Competition is a major issue for many of our companies, especially when it is related to innovation. The majority of companies reported that they *'work with their suppliers/subcontractors and customers because they have worked together before'* (mentioned 47 times). Furthermore, twenty-five companies mentioned that *'an atmosphere of trust existed prior to the actual product development'*. However, some managers reported that they had to trust their suppliers or customers, since they had no other option (mentioned 20 times).

When companies were asked if their customers made a contribution in knowledge or know-how towards developing one or more of the new products or services, 44% reported that they had. Moreover, 39% of managers said that they collaborated with their customers when developing these products. In addition, they gave information regarding how the idea for the new product arose (Table 3.7). Managers commented on a wide range of collaborative interactions, such as *'customers contribute to software solutions'*, *'we work with customers to improve customer systems'*, *'the customer made a contribution to printing press clutches and chemical pumps'*, *'the customer provides technical input and testing, and purchases the first production run'*, and so on.

Table 3.4: Relationships with Suppliers and Subcontractors

	Times mentioned			
	Cheltenham-Gloucester	Bristol-Bath	Swindon-M4	Total
Suppliers or subcontractors made a contribution to the firm's innovative process ...	10	7	10	27
... of which the firm collaborated with them when developing the new product	9	7	8	24

Total 61 firms
Source: Own survey.

Table 3.5: Geographical Location of Firms' Collaborating Suppliers and Subcontractors

	Times mentioned
South West of England	18
Another UK region	43
Another European country	18
Elsewhere	14

Total 61 firms
Source: Own survey.

Table 3.6: Destination of Sales

	Percentage of all sales
Locally/regionally	16
Nationally	53
Abroad	31

Total 53 firms (8 firms did not know)
Source: Own survey.

Table 3.7: Contributions to the Innovation Process by Firms' Customers

	Times mentioned
Of the 24 companies (39%) to which customers made a contribution, the idea arose primarily:	
- within the firm	31
- through an exchange of ideas with the collaborating customer	22
- from the collaborating customer	12
- from another source	2

Total 61 firms
Source: Own survey.

By investigating local and regional links, it becomes clear that the West of England agglomerations have developed a relatively high level of density of inter-firm interactions and close collaboration, based on both spatial proximity and trust. For instance, 59% of sampled firms reported that local links with firms providing services are important; just under half (49%) believed that links with suppliers or subcontractors are important; and 28% valued local links with competitors (Table 3.8).

An important indicator for the socialisation of managers and the cross-fertilisation of ideas and know-how is given in Table 3.9. In the theoretical concept of the innovative milieu, the so-called *cafeteria effect* is perhaps one of the most important factors in facilitating learning. The level of innovativeness of firms in regional agglomerations depends, therefore, on gathering knowledge through social interaction, which Malecki appropriately calls 'soft' networks (2002, p. 933). Table 3.9 indicates that 42% of the firms' managers never meet informally with managers or professionals from other local companies. However, half (49%) reported doing so occasionally, while a small proportion (9%) met frequently. This is in line with our earlier evidence that, for the majority of firms, internal sources of know-how (i.e. firms' staff and R&D departments) are more important for innovation than are external sources.

Table 3.8: The Importance of Local/Regional Links in the West of England

	% of firms[1]
Suppliers or subcontractors	49
Firms providing services	59
Research collaborators	15
Firms in same line of business	28

Total 61 firms

Note: More than one answer allowed.

Source: Own survey.

[1] On a scale from 0, indicating no opinion, to 7, indicating extremely important, only those firms rating local/regional links at least as high as 4 (moderately important) are included in the table above.

Table 3.9: Informal Contracts with Managers or Professionals from Other Local/Regional Companies

Frequency of contact	Cheltenham-Gloucester Number (% of all firms)		Bristol-Bath Number (%)		Swindon/M4 Number (%)		Total Number (%)	
Never	7	(12)	10	(16)	8	(13)	25	(41)
Occasionally	13	(21)	8	(15)	9	(15)	30	(51)
Frequently	1	(2)	2	(4)	2	(2)	5	(8)

Total 60 firms

Source: Own survey.

3.5 The Effect of Regional Specific Advantages on Firms' Development

In the South West of England, a great number of organisations exist at the regional level which are involved in supporting local or regional firms, and contribute to the innovation process. Such a network, consisting of public and private institutions, is called a *regional innovation system* (Braczyk et al., 1998; Cooke et al., 2000). In the South West, this includes organisations such as Chambers of Commerce, Business Links, Training Enterprise Councils, Further Education and Higher Education Institutions, Local Authorities, Professional Associations, and Regional Government (which now includes a number of previously independent development agencies), all of which encourage firms within the region to acquire a common culture of innovation. These organisations have been important in influencing the evolution and collective capacity for learning in the South West. Collective capacity takes the form of regional or local supply-chain networks, public-private partnerships, business and university collaborative networks, and Teaching Company Schemes, all of which help to improve the competitiveness of local SMEs through the diffusion of technology and know-how. The region's institutional environment facilitates learning at the levels of the individual worker, the individual firm, clusters of firms, and support institutions themselves. Since competitive success now depends on the production, use and diffusion of

Table 3.10: Regional Specific Advantages for Firms' Development

	At least 'moderately important'
Adequate road networks	87
Attractive local living environment for directors and managers	70
Availability of premises	56
Access to innovative people, technologies, creativity and ideas	55
The business atmosphere and reputation of the area	49
Access to airports	37
Availability of local regional universities	35
Availability of local research staff	16
Quality of local research staff	14

Total 61 companies
Note: Multiple responses allowed.
Source: Own survey.

knowledge, is there sufficient evidence to claim that we now live in a knowledge-based economy?

Tables 3.10 and 3.11 provide an insight into how innovative SMEs in this agglomeration rate regional resources that potentially affect the competitiveness of their business. The greatest resources for business effectiveness were perceived to be *'adequate road networks'*, *'attractive living environment'* and *'availability of premises'*. However, the resources that facilitate learning, such as *'access to innovative people, technologies, creativity and ideas'*, *'access to regional universities'*, and the *'availability'* and *'quality of local research staff'*, were not perceived to be of primary importance. Nevertheless, some regional universities, such as the University of Bath and the University of the West of England, are starting to exert an influence upon local technology-based SMEs. Generally speaking, the majority of our sample of SMEs felt that institutional support has a limited effect on promoting collaboration and learning. However, this is mainly due to the lack of awareness of SMEs regarding the institutional support on offer. The provision of local services provided by service firms and other organisations was highly rated. Maximum points were given to local legal services, followed by local accountancy companies, and postal and courier services (Table 3.12).

3.6 The Collective Learning Experience and Regional Channels of Knowledge Acquisition

Another important indication of the vitality of the West of England agglomeration is the reported rate of new local start-ups by former employees, and their linkages with the parent company. Table 3.13 indicates that the majority of firms had an independent start-up, while a quarter reported that they were a spin-off from an existing regional company. A further investigation into founders' origins, the results of which are shown

Table 3.11: Help or Advice Firms Received from Local Agencies (Government-Sponsored or Otherwise) over the Last Five Years, and Rating of the Usefulness of Such Help/Advice

			Rating	
	Times mentioned	*Good*	*Moderate*	*Poor*
Training and Enterprise Council	19	8	9	2
District or Local Council	18	6	7	5
Chamber of Commerce	27	16	6	5
Business Link	33	16	13	4
Enterprise/Development Agency	11	5	3	3
European Innovation Relay Centre	4	0	1	3
Regional Universities/HE Institutions	21	12	7	2

Total 61 firms

Note: Multiple responses allowed.

Source: Own survey.

Table 3.12: Help and Support in Provision and Quality of Local Services in the West of England

Services provided	*% of firms using local services for 50% or more of their needs*	*Ranking*	*of Local (%)*	*Services*
		Good	*Moderate*	*Poor*
Banks	87	66	28	6
Venture Capital Providers	15	56	22	22
Accountancy	52	78	19	3
Legal Services	72	84	14	2
Marketing/Market Research	25	60	40	0
Advertising	39	63	29	8
Management Consultancy	18	64	18	18

in Table 3.14, reveals that the majority had been working in other regional companies, rather than being self-employed or employed by a university or other research institutions. Although the majority of founders reported that they possessed research and managerial experience, the findings imply a rather limited diffusion of research expertise and technological innovation from regional research institutions. Nevertheless, a further investigation into the origins of firms' latest research or managerial recruits reveals that a large number of such staff came from a local or regional company, or from a local or regional university (Table 3.15). As already noted, the literature of the innovative milieu draws special attention to the skilled labour mobility within this milieu. Skilled labour is considered to be fundamental in the diffusion of tacit expertise and technological know-how. In this study, 22 company managers (representing 36% of the sample) reported that, during the last five years, some skilled employees who had left the company had formed their own business, and the majority of these businesses were located in the West of England (Table 3.16). In addition, 18 of these managers, representing 30% of sample, reported that links exist

Table 3.13: Regional and Local Channels of Knowledge Acquisition of High-Technology SMEs in the West of England: New Firm Start-Ups and Local Entrepreneurship

Firms' origins	Number of firms	%
An independent start-up	35	60
A set-up by another firm	8	14
A spin-off from an existing company	15	26

Total 58 firms
Source: Own survey.

Table 3.14: Owners'/Founders' Origins

Type of employment	Firm is 15 years old or less	Firm is more than 15 years old	Total	
Self-employed or unemployed	3	1	4	
Working in another company	29	12	41	8
Working in a university	0	1	1	
Employed by another institution	1	2	3	

Total 49 firms
Source: Own survey.

Table 3.15: Origins of Firms' Latest Research/Engineering/Management Staff

Source mentioned	Times mentioned
Other local/regional companies/organisations	34
Other UK companies/organisations	26
Overseas companies/organisations	2
A local/regional university (i.e. Bath, Bristol or UWE)	12
Other UK university	13
Overseas university	10

Total 61 firms
Note: Respondents may have identified more than one location or institution.
Source: Own survey.

Table 3.16: New Local Start-Ups by Former Employees and Existing Linkages

	Cheltenham-Gloucester	Bristol-Bath	Swindon/M4	Total Number	Total %
Number of new start-ups by former employees ...	6	10	6	22	36
... of which established in the locality or in the rest of the South West ...	3	8	6	17	28
... of which continuing links with the 'parent' company in the form of informal links	1	6	4	11	18
... or in the form of formal links	1	1	3	7	11

Total 61 companies
Source: Own survey.

between their company and other local/regional companies through staff who have moved between them. Furthermore, the majority of the 22 companies (representing 16% of the total sample) considered these links to be very important, rather than fairly important or not important. These findings support the view that there is some interchange of highly qualified staff within the West of England agglomeration, and local technology-intensive SMEs are benefiting from knowledge and expertise found in the region's skilled human capital.

Our findings indicate that the majority of technology-intensive SMEs in the West of England are more likely to develop their innovations regionally, rather than nationally or abroad through subcontracting or through a subsidiary, and a significant number of them are becoming breakthrough innovators. The majority of such firms emphasise the importance of internal sources of innovation (i.e. staff and/or R&D department). However, as Keeble et al. point out, internal innovativeness suggests that regional collective processes are present in the form of previous local spin-offs or recruitment of local skilled workforce (Keeble, 1999, p. 327). High-technology firms also exhibit high R&D intensity, have a large proportion of skilled, managerial and scientific staff, adopt innovative inter-firm practices extensively, and are likely to collaborate in terms of innovation with local, regional, national and even foreign customers and suppliers. The above analysis suggests that the regional/local context and support institutions exert a significant influence on the nature and extent of the innovative activities of technology-intensive SMEs. At the same time, however, the wider national, European and even global innovation networks are also important for bringing to regional agglomerations the technological expertise that is needed for the development and commercialisation of major innovations.

Notes

[1] The R&D intensity of the sample companies is well above that of the UK average (4.9). The UK R&D intensity appears to be more comparable with France (4.9), Germany (6.0) and Japan (5.4) than the overall OECD average (7.9). DTI, (1998), *'The 1998 UK R&D Scoreboard'*, London: DTI.

Chapter 4:

Innovation in the Singapore-Johor

Agglomeration

This chapter presents the results of the empirical investigation carried out in the Singapore-Johor cross-border area - a suitable case for analysis, since the pre-conditions for collective learning are present, in the existence of a highly skilled workforce, first-class infrastructure, a large number of TNCs, and many spin-offs of high-technology companies. The area analysed not only constitutes the two most significant corners of the afore-mentioned *SIJORI growth triangle*, but is also one of the most important agglomerations of high-technology companies in South-East Asia as a whole. The objective of this chapter, as well as its structure, is similar to that of the previous chapter: namely, to present an analysis of the different types of interactions among regional innovative SMEs and other regional or local economic actors, and to compare them within the context of the innovative milieu 'model'. A further aim is to establish the existence of collective learning and firms' linkages, the effectiveness of support institutions, and the role of regional resources in facilitating learning and collaborative interactions among the agglomeration's SMEs.

The core of the field research was a large number of interviews with local firms, decision-makers and experts. The research analysis draws mainly from the afore-mentioned European theoretical concept of the innovative milieu, as well as clusters and industrial districts, and the growth triangles which are specific to Asia.

4.1 The Profile of Innovative Regional Firms

The fieldwork was carried out in Singapore and Johor Bahru, in both of which there is a critical mass of spatially concentrated high-technology firms and institutions. The survey was based on structured interviews of the managers of 30 SMEs, and a number of open interviews with some regional decision-makers and experts.[1] The sample of 30 high-technology firms - 20 from Singapore (mainly from the industrial areas and estates of Jurong, Ang Moh Kio, Pasir Ris, Bedok, Kent Ridge and Bukit Merah), and 10 from Johor Bahru (Tebrau I, II and IV industrial estates) - was randomly drawn from trade directories (see Figure 4.1). In particular, for the Singapore part of the survey, companies were selected from the latest available edition of the Directory of Electronics Industry and the Directory of Engineering and Machinery Industry. For the Johor agglomeration, company directories were kindly supplied by Johor Technopark, a subsidiary of the Johor Corporation.

Before interpreting the results, one additional limitation of the data needs to be taken into account. It is possible that, with the majority of managers being Chinese, traditional courtesy might have introduced a degree of bias into the survey data, as there is often a reluctance to give negative answers to an interviewer. However, this is not likely to have significantly affected the results.

The structure of the sampled firms, showing size and location, is shown in Table 4.1. Half of the firms (50%) are small businesses in high-technology sectors employing less than 100 employees, while the great majority (87%) are SMEs employing less than 250 employees. The firms are a representative sample of innovative companies in the Singapore-Johor agglomeration.

Table 4.1: Size and Location of Sampled Firms used in the 1999 Survey in Singapore-Johor

Location of firms	<50 employees	50-100 employees	101-250 employees	>250 employees	Total
Singapore	10	3	7	0	20
Johor Bahru	2	0	4	4	10
Total (%)	12 (40%)	3 (10%)	11 (37%)	4 (13%)	30

Total 30 firms
Source: Own survey.

Before embarking on a more detailed picture of the innovative milieu characteristics identified[2], some general characteristics of the sampled firms should be considered:

* The average age of the firms is 10 years, the youngest being three years old and the oldest 28 years old. The majority (55%) are young firms, established after 1990.
* Approximately half of the firms belong to the electronics and telecommunications sector, one third to the engineering sector, and one tenth to the electronic service sector (mostly trading or regional headquarters of foreign companies). The remainder are contract or assembly manufacturers, especially within the Malaysian sample.
* The majority (60%) of the firms are regionally owned companies, rather than a subsidiary or part of a group of companies. The Singapore sample had the highest number of indigenous companies[3]. From our interviews with the managers of such companies, we identified that some businesses were established by people who had had previous experience in a similar line of business and had their origins in Singapore or Malaysia.

The sample of firms represents a considerable part of the regional economy, as they employ approximately 3,900 workers (average 129) and generate a turnover of almost S$1 billion (£370 million). Firms were asked to report the percentage of their employees who are designated as either scientists/engineers or administrators/managers. The average percentage was 32, irrespective of company size but dependent on industrial sectors. This is only half of the percentage found in the West of England. Companies involved in electronics and telecommunications manufacturing and services, however, reported an above average percentage of skilled workforce. Once more, the location of companies appears to be significant. There is a greater concentration of skilled workforce in Singapore than in the Johor Bahru area.

Figure 4.1: Clustering of High-Technology SMEs in Singapore-Johor Bahru

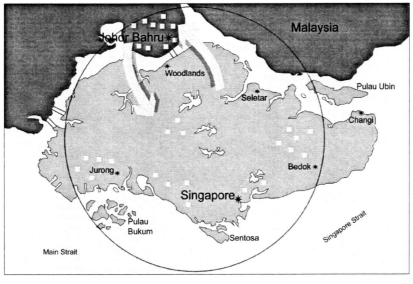

☐   Sample SMEs

An indication of how our sample of firms performed during the last five years is given by the changes in the number of employees and in business turnover, as well as the reported level of profits for their latest financial year. These changes show that the majority of our sampled companies are not performing well (although this is partly attributable to the financial crisis of 1997-8). For instance, 67% of firms reported that they decreased their number of employees, and 77% their turnover, while 10% reported static employment growth. Only 23% of firms reported an increase in employment or turnover respectively.

4.2. Regional Innovators and their Sources of Innovation

The survey shows that of the 18 regionally owned companies, which represent 60% of the sample, 10 of them (or 33%) have an R&D department, and all these departments are located in Singapore. In addition, seven of the companies reported that they had patented a product or a process innovation during the last five years, representing 23% of the total sample. (This is much lower than in the West of England, where, as mentioned in the previous chapter, 34% of companies had patented an innovation during the same period.) Moreover, six (20%) of the regionally owned companies reported *breakthrough* innovations (i.e. new products or services) with an application to semi-manufactured and consumer electronics.

The twelve externally controlled companies (40% of the total sample) do not play a significant part (at least directly) in the innovative performance of the area. Only two

Table 4.2: Innovation Output of Firms in Manufacturing and Services (1994-1999) in the Singapore and Johor Bahru Area, and Average R&D Intensity in 1998

	Firms with innovations	Firms with no innovations	All firms
Number of firms	7	23	30
... in Singapore (with breakthrough innovations[1])	6 (6)	14	20
... in Johor Bahru (with breakthrough innovations[1])	1 (0)	9	10
Average R&D spending in 1998 as % of sales[2]	24%	5.4%	9.8%

Total 30 firms
Source: Own survey.
[1] These include development of laser technology, electronic connectors, semiconductor technology, digital cable technology, international data compression technology and a wide area data application.
[2] Arithmetic average.

of them (7%) have their own R&D department located in Singapore or Johor Bahru, and only one has patented a product or a process innovation during the last five years. Furthermore, no externally controlled company has produced a *breakthrough* innovation (see Table 4.2). This appears to reinforce the belief that multinationals are less likely to undertake R&D outside their home area than are indigenous companies. As Gertler et al. have asserted in their study of manufacturing firms in Ontario, Canada, '...innovations undertaken by multinational firms in their foreign operations are relatively superficial, involving either customization to meet the needs of individual customers, or adaptation to suit prevailing local, regional or national market tastes...' (Gertler et al., 2000, p. 703).

An additional indication of the level of innovative activity in the agglomeration is the amount spent by firms on R&D. In 1998, the average R&D intensity was a robust 9.8% (compared to the 6.3% found in the West of England). In addition, new products and services accounted for exactly a quarter of the firms' sales in the previous year, indicating the importance of new innovative products. The alternative method of finding evidence for a firm's innovative activity, through its purchase of different types of advanced equipment or machinery, licensed products, and advanced software during the last three years, shows that the vast majority of them (87%) have made such purchases.

With the exception of four firms in Johor which sell all of their products within their own national market, the sampled firms export on average three quarters of their products or services. (For the sake of simplicity, an export is a sale to countries beyond the borders of both Singapore and Malaysia.)

As in the West of England survey, firms' managers were asked to report the main sources of know-how - i.e. their R&D department, staff, other companies, government departments, and universities (Figure 4.2) - leading to their most important

Table 4.3: Principal Input of Learning for the Most Important Innovations for Firms in the Singapore-Johor Bahru Area

Learning input	Times mentioned	
Internal source: firm's R&D and/or design departments	17*	
firm's staff	12	
Total		**29**
External source: other company(ies)	11	
government department	4	
university	3	
other (associations, Web sites, etc.)	4	
Total		**22**

Total 30 firms
Source: Own survey.
Note: More than one answer allowed.
*including parent company's overseas R&D department (7 times)

Figure 4.2: Sources of Learning in Singapore-Johor

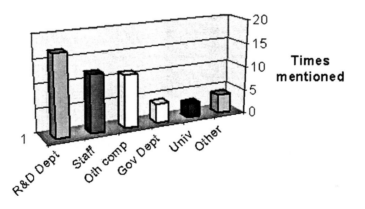

innovations. Again it appears that internal sources are more important for innovation than external ones (Table 4.3). However, unlike the West of England, where the firm's staff is the most important source, in the Singapore-Johor area it is the R&D departments (including the overseas departments of firms not regionally owned). External sources are also important, in particular relations with other companies, including customers, suppliers, subcontractors and competitors.

4.3 Regional Collaboration in Product and Process Development

Our earlier review of the theoretical conceptualisation of the innovative milieu postulates that collective learning requires high levels of interaction and exchanges of technological information, as well as collaboration in product development between firms and institutions in the regional agglomeration. For this reason, the sampled companies were asked to report whether they had a partner collaborating in the development of one of their latest new products or processes. Figure 4.3 shows that firms' customers are the most important collaborating partners, followed by suppliers. Although universities, agencies and consultants do not emerge as important collaborators, many firms' managers expressed a distinct interest in developing relationships with local universities and other public research institutions.

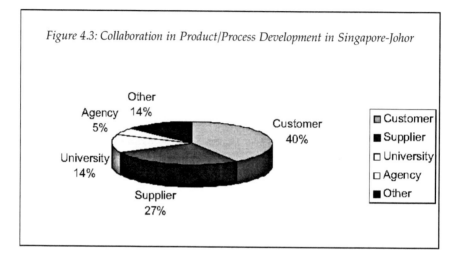

Figure 4.3: Collaboration in Product/Process Development in Singapore-Johor

4.4 Inter-firm Linkages, Networks and Collaboration

One of the most important considerations in our survey is to analyse the linkages, networks and modes of collaboration of high-technology SMEs in the Singapore-Johor area. How do innovative firms in the Singapore-Johor agglomeration interact with each other? What type of relations, linkages and transnational networks exist between Singaporean, Malaysian and multinational companies? Are regional institutions instrumental in supporting innovation, as are their counterparts in the West of England?

The majority of the sampled firms (54%) stated that they purchase their raw materials, basic services, components and advanced services at the local/regional level, although an unspecified amount of raw materials and components are imported. For the Singapore-Johor firms (which, as a group, rated suppliers as the second most important collaborators in innovation), local suppliers appear to be marginally more important than those located in the rest of Malaysia or overseas. Moreover, firms reported that relations with their main suppliers are good; only one third of firms had problems regarding service, or with the availability, price or quality of materials, in their relationship with suppliers. The survey results, which shed further light on inter-firm linkages, networks and forms of collaboration, are presented in Tables 4.4 to 4.8.

Table 4.4: Relationships with Suppliers and Subcontractors

	Times mentioned		
	Singapore	Johor Bahru	Total
Suppliers or subcontractors made a contribution to the firm's innovative process ...	7	2	9
... of which the firm collaborated with them when developing the new product	5	2	7

Total 30 firms
Source: Own survey.

For instance, the vast majority (77%) of the sampled firms' managers believe that meeting and discussing business with their suppliers/subcontractors is important for their company. In addition, one third felt that their company had made a significant contribution in knowledge or know-how in developing a new product or service with their suppliers or subcontractors. This included collaboration in the development of cellular telephones, laser instruments, medical and military equipment, electronics, compression technology for the Internet, and development of cables for electronic applications.

The most common type of linkage among regional firms is informal relationships[4]. For example, 30% of firms reported that they have frequent contact with their suppliers, 50% have occasional contact, and the remaining 20% have none at all. These informal relationships normally come about because of spatial proximity (mentioned 15 times), meetings or seminars organised by local associations or organisations (mentioned 7 times), or social occasions (mentioned 6 times). As in the West of England, they take place in a wide range of networking arrangements, such as meetings organised by government departments, hospitality dinners and lunches, and exhibitions and trade fairs. Surprisingly, family connections - normally so important for some of the ethnic groups represented within the agglomeration - were rarely reported to play an important role for firms (mentioned only twice).

Again, in this regional cluster, we encounter the paradox of firms competing as well as co-operating. Competition has been a major issue for many of our companies, especially within the electronics sector, where frequent contact with competitors is a consequence of close physical proximity. The majority of companies reported that they work *'with our suppliers/subcontractors because we have worked together before'* (mentioned 12 times), that *'the supplier/subcontractor was recommended to us by others'* (mentioned 9 times), and that *'an atmosphere of trust existed prior to the actual product development'* (mentioned 8 times). However, some managers reported that they had to *'trust our suppliers or customers since we had no other option'* (mentioned 4 times). This was especially so for contract manufacturing companies dependent on TNCs. When firms were asked if their suppliers/subcontractors made a contribution in knowledge or know-how towards developing one or more of their new products or services, 30%

Table 4.5: Contributions to the innovation Process by Firms' Suppliers or Subcontractors

	Times mentioned
Of the 9 companies (30%) to which suppliers made a contribution, the idea arose primarily:	
- within the firm	11
- through an exchange of ideas with the collaborating supplier	1
- from the collaborating supplier	1
- from another source	3

Total 30 firms
Source: Own survey.

Table 4.6: Geographical Location of Firms' Collaborating Suppliers or Subcontractors

	Times mentioned
Singapore	17
State of Johor	14
Other Malaysian state	8
Other ASEAN member state	4
Japan	13
Rest of Asia	6
Europe	14
United States	10
Elsewhere	3

Total 30 firms
Source: Own survey.

Table 4.7: Destination of Sales

	Percentage of all sales
Locally/regionally/nationally	46
Abroad[1]	54

Total 30 firms
Source: Own survey.
[1] That is, countries beyond the borders of both Singapore and Malaysia.

Table 4.8: Contributions to the Innovation Process by Firms' Customers

	Times mentioned[1]
Of the 22 companies (73% of the sample) to which customers made a contribution, the idea arose primarily:	
- within the firm	6
- through an exchange of ideas with the collaborating customer	7
- from the collaborating customer	12
- from another source	2

Total 30 firms
Source: Own survey.
[1] Multiple responses permitted.

Table 4.9: Geographical Location of Firms' Collaborating Customers

	Times mentioned
Singapore	20
State of Johor	8
Other Malaysian state	11
Japan	9
Other ASEAN member state	1
Rest of Asia	4
Europe	9
United States	11
Elsewhere	1

Total 30 firms
Source: Own survey.

Table 4.10: Contributionof Collaborating Customers

	Times mentioned
Providing expertise or knowledge	12
Supplying components	8
Supplying capital goods (computers, machinery, etc.)	6
Developing an innovation	6
Providing scientific input or insights	5
Taking part in the production of the product	3
Placing staff at the firm's service	2
Other	4

Total 30 firms
Source: Own survey.

Table 4.11: The Importance of Local/Regional Links in Singapore-Johor

	% of firms[1]
Suppliers and customers	90
Firms providing services	87
Research collaborators	43
Firms in same line of business	53

Total 30 firms

Source: Own survey.

[1] On a scale from 0, indicating no opinion, to 7, indicating extremely important, only those firms rating local/regional links at least as high as 4 (moderately important) are included in the table above.

Table 4.12: Informal Contacts with Managers or Professionals from Other Local/Regional Companies

Frequency of contact	Singapore		Johor Bahru		Total	
	Number	(% of all firms)	Number	(%)	Number	(%)
Never	1	(3)	0	(0)	1	(3)
Occasionally	12	(40)	7	(24)	19	(64)
Frequently	7	(23)	3	(10)	10	(33)

Total 30 firms

Source: Own survey.

said that their customers did indeed make a contribution. Moreover, 23% of firms' managers reported that they collaborated with their suppliers when they were developing the above products. However, when they were asked the source of the idea for the new product or service, the majority said that it came primarily from within their own company (mentioned 11 times), rather than through an exchange of ideas with their collaborating suppliers/subcontractors (mentioned only once) or through an idea developed exclusively by them (again, mentioned only once) (Table 4.5).

The sampled firms displayed stronger interactions with their customers than with their suppliers. This emphasises the importance of customers for the firms' survival, as well as the fact that they make a greater contribution to knowledge acquisition and know-how than do suppliers. On average, 54% of firms' output is exported abroad (Table 4.7), and for the companies in Singapore in particular, the majority of customers are based abroad. However, if we take into account the output of the contract manufacturers, whose products are exported indirectly by their transnational manufacturers, then exports are much higher.

When firms were asked if their customers made a contribution in knowledge or know-how towards developing one or more of their new products or services, the great majority (73%) said that this was the case. This included contributions to new or improved products in cellular telephony (2), electronics/semiconductors (4), automation (1), and precision engineering (1). Moreover, 40% of firms' managers reported that they entered into full collaboration with their customers when they were developing the above products. In addition, they provided information on how the idea for the new product arose (Table 4.8). Managers of the smallest indigenous SMEs commented on a wide range of collaborative interactions, such as *'we worked with our customers in the production of this new product', 'Philips and IBM taught us how to make new components for them'*, and so on. When the managers were asked how often their company exchanges ideas or discusses problems with their customers, the majority (63%) said often, 33% occasionally, and only 4% never. Furthermore, almost all of the managers (97%) believed that meeting and discussing business with their customers is important for their company.

Firms' relationships with their customers usually came about through meetings organised by local associations (mentioned 12 times). Spatial proximity was also important (mentioned 10 times), followed by social occasions, while family connections were only mentioned once. Moreover, many firms emphasised the importance of existing business or industrial relations, and the activity of their marketing managers in establishing links with their most important customers. Table 4.9 shows that, for the majority of firms, their most important collaborating customers are found locally, regionally or nationally (i.e. in Singapore, the State of Johor, or another Malaysian state). However, a significant number of firms' customers are American, followed by Japanese and Europeans.

The survey also identified the various industry affiliations of the firms' customers. They are mainly in electronics/semiconductors (14 cases), telecommunications (3), consumer electronics (3), and automation/precision engineering (2).

Table 4.10 shows the different kinds of contribution made by the firms' customers to the development of a new product or process. The most frequently quoted was expertise and knowledge, followed by the supply of components or capital goods.

The most common type of linkages between the sampled firms and their customers was informal relationships (mentioned 13 times), as was the case with regard to suppliers. However, a formal structure for the collaboration agreement in the form of a contract was mentioned by 11 firms. In our sample, 37% of companies reported that they have frequent contact with their customers, 47% occasional contact, and the remaining 16% none at all. The majority of companies reported that they work *'with our customers because we have worked together before'* (mentioned 13 times), that *'the customer was recommended to us by others'* (10 times), and that *'an atmosphere of trust existed prior to the actual product development'* (again, 10 times). However, some managers reported having to *'trust our customers since we have no other option'* (mentioned 5 times). Again, this was especially so for contract manufacturing companies dependent on TNCs.

By investigating local and regional links, it becomes clear that the Singapore-Johor agglomeration has developed a relatively high level of density of inter-firm interactions and close collaboration based on both spatial proximity and trust[5]. As we have seen, the innovative milieux are, in theory, loci of trust-based linkages between firms. According to De Propis, there is an array of factors (social, economic, cultural and historical) which could explain the development of trust-based culture in a regional agglomeration and which affect the flexibility of such milieux (2001, p. 746). For instance, local links with suppliers, subcontractors or customers are considered important by 90% of the sampled firms, links with companies providing services by 87%, and those with research collaborators and competitors by 43% and 53% respectively (Table 4.11). When firms were asked to disclose if they have close links with other firms in their locality or the rest of the Singapore-Johor area, 63% reported that they did. The majority of such linkages were with firms in high-technology manufacturing and services.

An indication of the degree to which managers socialise and thereby exchange ideas and know-how is given in Table 4.12. It seems the *cafeteria effect* is more apparent in the Singapore-Johor agglomeration than in the West of England. The majority of managers (64%) reported that they meet occasionally with managers or professionals from other local companies, while as many as one third (33%) do so frequently. Only 3% never meet informally. The managers of the Japanese-owned companies in particular stated that they meet regularly, at the various functions organised by the local Japanese communi

4.5 The Effect of Regional Specific Advantages on Firms' Development

Both in Singapore and in the State of Johor, a number of institutions exist which are involved in supporting local companies. These include well-known entities such as the Economic Development Board (EDB), the Productivity and Standards Board (PSD), and the Confederation of Industries (all in Singapore), and the Johor Corporation and the Economic Planning Unit in the State of Johor. Chambers of Commerce, colleges, universities, local authorities and industry associations are also part of this support network. The infrastructure for influencing the evolution and collective capacity of the Singapore-Johor agglomeration takes the form of public-private partnerships, training of employees, and business and university collaborative networks that help to improve the competitiveness of local SMEs through the diffusion of technology and know-how.

Tables 4.13 and 4.14 provide an insight into how regional innovative SMEs rate regional resources that affect their business competitiveness: access to infrastructure facilities, the business atmosphere and reputation of the area, access to innovative people, technologies, creativity and ideas, attractive local living environment, availability of premises and labour supply, availability of local regional universities, and quality and availability of local research staff. Managers in both Singapore and Johor Bahru reported that the two most important resources for their business effectiveness were '*access to infrastructure facilities*', and '*the business atmosphere and the reputation of the area*'. However, whereas the Singaporean managers rated '*access to innovative people, technologies, creativity and ideas*' as the next most important, those in Johor Bahru quoted '*proximity to Singapore's infrastructure facilities*'. Other resources that facilitate learning, such as '*availability*' and '*quality of local research/engineering staff*' were also considered to be of importance. Although '*availability of local universities*' was only

Table 4.13: Regional Specific Advantages for Firms' Development

	At least 'moderately important'
Access to infrastructure facilities (airports/ports/roads)	93
The business atmosphere and reputation of the area	90
Proximity to Singapore's infrastructure facilities[1]	80
Access to innovative people, technologies, creativity and ideas	73
Availability of local research/engineering staff	70
Quality of local research/engineering staff	67
Availability of premises	67
Attractive local living environment for directors and managers	60
Availability of local regional universities	50
Availability of abundant labour supply in Johor[1]	40

Total 30 firms
Note: Multiple responses allowed.
Source: Own survey.
[1] Only companies based in Johor.

Table 4.14: Help or Advice Firms Received from Local Agencies (Government-Sponsored or Otherwise) over the Last Five Years, and Rating of the Usefulness of such Help/Advice

	Times mentioned	*Good*	Rating *Moderate*	*Poor*
Professional Associations	6	1	5	0
Local Council/Authorities	7	2	4	1
Chamber of Commerce	7	3	3	1
National Organisations/Agencies, Enterprise Board or Development Agency	23	16	6	1
(Regional) Universities or other HE Institution	7	4	1	2

Total 30 firms
Note: Multiple responses allowed.
Source: Own survey.

rated moderately important, some institutions, such as the National University of Singapore, Nanyang University, and the University of Technology of Malaysia in Johor, are nevertheless starting to exert an influence upon local technology-based SMEs.

The majority of the sampled SMEs reported that institutional support has a limited effect on promoting collaboration and collective learning. However, this is mainly due to their lack of awareness as to what support is on offer. Nevertheless, the provision of local services provided by other firms was highly praised. Maximum points were given to local courier services, followed by venture capital providers (although very few firms used the latter).

Table 4.15: Help and Support in Provision and Quality of Local Services in Singapore-Johor Area

Service provided	% of firms using local services for 50% or more of their needs	Ranking	of local %	services
		Good	Moderate	Poor
Banks	97	69	24	7
Courier Services	90	93	7	0
Accountancy	87	58	38	4
Computer Services	80	58	38	4
Recruitment/Personnel Services	73	27	68	5
Legal Services	70	62	33	5
Design/Printing Services	65	65	30	5
Advertising	47	36	57	7
Management Consultancy	37	45	36	19
Marketing/Market Research	27	25	75	0
Public Relations	17	60	40	0
Venture Capital Providers	13	75	25	0

Total 30 firms
Source: Own survey.

4.6 The Collective Learning Experience and Regional Channels of Knowledge Acquisition

As noted in the literature review, collective learning is attributed to the mobility of the local labour market, which accumulates its own knowledge and experience. The sampled firms reported that the average percentage of labour turnover within the last five years was 14%, although for companies in Johor it was much higher (20%) than for companies in Singapore (11%). This local cumulative knowledge may be grasped by local actors (particularly SMEs), and is the source of local dynamic comparative advantage. As the GREMI group postulates, when local actors appropriate collective learning and turn it into profits, an *innovative milieu* emerges. Therefore, one of the most important aims of this study is to identify and measure the extent and importance of knowledge acquisition and learning within regionally based high-technology SMEs. A further aim is to identify whether the Singapore-Johor agglomeration is an innovative milieu, or a potential innovative area.

A detailed examination of the collective learning experience and regional channels of knowledge acquisition presents a contrasting picture. The vast majority of the sampled firms are either independent start-ups or subsidiaries of foreign companies. There were only four firms, representing just 13% of the sample, which are the result of spin-offs from another local/regional firm or institution. This low rate of spin-off was confirmed when firms reported on the origins of their owner(s) or founder(s). The overwhelming majority of entrepreneurs had been employed previously in a company, or had been self-employed (most commonly working in a family-owned company), while only two had been employed in a government research laboratory or research institution. However, the majority of such entrepreneurs in the high-technology

Table 4.16: Regional and Local Channels of Knowledge Acquisition of High-Technology SMEsin the Singapore-Johor Area: New Firm Start-Ups and Local Entrepreneurship

Firms' origins	Number of firms	%
An independent start-up	16	54
A set-up by another firm	10	33
A spin-off from an existing company	4	13

Total 30 firms
Source: Own survey.

Table 4.17: Owners'/Founders' Origins

Type of employment	Times mentioned	%
Self-employed or unemployed	5	27
Working in another company	12	63
Working in a university	0	0
Working in a government research laboratory	1	5
Employed by another institution	1	5

Total 19 firms
Source: Own survey.

Table 4.18: Owners'/Founders' Experience and Qualifications

Type of Experience and/or qualifications	Number of owners/founders
Research/engineering experience	11
Research/engineering qualifications	13
Managerial experience	14
Managerial qualifications	10

Total 30 firms
Source: Own survey.

industries possessed research/engineering, as well as managerial, experience and qualifications. Yet it is the top scientific/engineering or managerial staff of a company, together with the entrepreneur himself, who have the potential for making a significant contribution to the firm's innovative activities. When managers were asked to state the origins of their latest research/engineering or managerial staff, they reported that the majority of their most recent knowledge-skilled recruits had been working in another local/regional company (mentioned 19 times), or had graduated from an overseas

Table 4.19: Origins of Firms' Latest Research/Engineering/Management Staff

Source mentioned	Times mentioned
Other local/regional companies/organisations	19
Other Malaysian companies/organisations	5
Overseas companies/organisations	7
A local/regional university (i.e. NUS, Nanyang or UTM)	7
Other Malaysian university	3
Overseas university	9

Total 30 firms

Note: Respondents may have identified more than one location or institution.
Source: Own survey.

Table 4.20: New Local Start-Ups by Former Employees and Existing Linkages

	Singapore	Johor Bahru	Total Number	Total %
Number of new start-ups by former employees ...	13	2	15	50
... of which established in the locality or in the rest of Singapore-Johor ...	11	2	13	43
... of which continuing links with the 'parent' company in the form of informal links	7	0	7	23
... or in the form of formal links	4	1	5	17

Total 30 firms
Source: Own survey.

university (mentioned 9 times), or been employed by an overseas company (mentioned 7 times). A further investigation into the nationality of graduates from overseas universities and recruits from overseas companies revealed that the majority were highly skilled staff brought in from China and India to work in the high-tech sectors. It appears that these immigrants make a major contribution to technology acquisition in the Singapore-Johor area.

Another important indication of the vitality of the Singapore-Johor agglomeration is the reported new local start-ups by former employees, and their linkages with their parent company. Fifteen company managers (representing a healthy 50% of our sample) reported that during the last five years some employees who had left the company had formed their own business, and the majority of these businesses were located in the Singapore-Johor area. This figure is higher than the 36% reported in the West of England. More importantly, the majority of these new entrepreneurs continued to have formal or informal links with their parent firm, implying that information sharing, generation of trust, and learning is taking place. This is evidence that local entrepreneurs are taking advantage of the collective learning present locally. In addition, ten companies, representing 33% of the sample, reported that links exist between their company and other local/regional companies because of staff who have moved between these companies. Furthermore, the majority of these companies (representing 23% of the total sample) considered these links to be very important, rather than fairly important or not important at all.

Our findings indicate that the indigenous high-technology SMEs in the Singapore-Johor cross-border area are more likely to perform innovative activities locally, whereas foreign-owned subsidiaries depend on their parent company's overseas R&D department. Both indigenous and foreign-owned SMEs draw primarily from internal sources of innovation (mainly from their R&D departments and their staff), followed closely by external sources (mainly from other companies through collaboration in innovation). It appears that the learning behaviour of indigenous high-technology SMEs in the Singapore-Johor agglomeration has been influenced by the long legacy of dominance by foreign-owned firms, which has profoundly shaped their innovative practices. Despite this legacy of dependency on foreign firms for know-how and innovativeness, the indigenous high-technology SMEs are starting to develop significant innovative capabilities in the electronics and precision engineering sectors.

However, all high-technology SMEs in the sample exhibit high R&D intensity, and one third of their workforce consists of skilled, managerial, engineering and scientific staff. More importantly, they extensively adopt innovative inter-firm practices, and their customers, suppliers and subcontractors contribute significantly to the firms' innovation processes. The majority of firms' collaborators are situated either in Singapore or in the State of Johor, followed closely by foreign collaborators from Europe, Japan and the United States. Moreover, regional collective processes are present, given the high frequency of socialisation of firms' managers, movement of labour and recruitment of local skilled workforce, and new local start-ups and spin-offs from existing firms.

An attempt was made to measure the degree of local embeddedness of firms by asking them to rank the importance of regional resources to their competitiveness, as well as the usefulness of the support offered by local/regional support institutions. The analysis suggests that geographical proximity is clearly significant, as the regional/local context and support institutions in the Singapore-Johor agglomeration exert considerable influence on the nature and extent of the innovative activities of technology-intensive SMEs. However, a further observation should be made before progressing to chapter 5, where the main characteristics of knowledge-intensive SMEs in the West of England and Singapore-Johor agglomerations are compared in more detail. Firms or institutions located outside the agglomeration, and in particular in Europe, Japan or the United States, appear to be important sources of innovative ideas for SMEs in the Singapore-Johor area. Given the fact that the Singapore-Johor firms sell most of their output abroad, it would be misleading to characterise firms' innovative relations and knowledge acquisition as exclusively local or regional. It is becoming apparent that the global markets and global innovation networks are emerging as significant facilitators of learning for innovation for small high-technology South-East Asian firms.

Notes

[1] Logistical and financial constraints did not allow the author to include the same number of firms as in the West of England. Nevertheless, the 30 firms interviewed and surveyed provided adequate data to enable identification of an explanatory model for testing their learning behaviour.

[2] In a previous publication, the author examined some of the main points discussed in more detail here; see, Konstadakopulos, (2000c).

[3] Three major business groups dominate the high-technology sectors in South-East Asia: manufacturing-based TNCs, government-linked corporations, and indigenous (mostly family) firms. Historically, many of the family firms started as traders and merchants, then moved into real estate or became suppliers of products or services to TNCs. Ethnic Chinese, who adopt a paternalistic and intuitive style of management, control the majority of them. Such firms usually depend upon dense social networks composed of family members, friends and government officials (Yeung, 2000b, pp. 211-213).

[4] The reliance on informal personal relations (*guanxi*), particularly within South-East Asian Chinese business circles, is well documented, and thus there is no need to expand here.

[5] Chinese businesses in particular consider that trust (*xinyong*) is an organisational principle, embedded in a system of interpersonal social relationships, and not a legal duty (Hamilton, 1998, p. 62).

Chapter 5:

A Comparative Analysis of Patterns of Learning Behaviour and Co-operation in the West of England and Singapore-Johor

The partial quantitative analyses of fieldwork data presented in the previous two chapters indicate that a great deal of further information can be extracted and evaluated. With the objective of investigating further the innovative behaviour of SMEs in the West of England and Singapore-Johor, the sample surveys were analysed using several statistical techniques. The quantitative analyses of the results of the sample surveys complement and cross-reference the qualitative analyses of the collective effects deriving from the firms' interviews. In addition, these results are compared, and their similarities and differences analysed. In particular, an attempt is made to provide answers to the following two questions:

Do the West of England and the Singapore-Johor agglomerations match the ideal model of the innovative milieu as described in the literature review in chapter 2?

What are the most important similarities and/or differences between high-technology SMEs in the two agglomerations?

In order to provide a satisfactory answer to the above questions, statistical analysis was undertaken on the data sets of the two-sample survey. Two large matrices (61 rows x 180 columns, and 30 rows x 180 columns), containing over 10,000 and 5,000 cells of information respectively, were constructed. However, the vast amount of raw data made simplification necessary. For this simplification, a principal component factor analysis for each set of the survey data was employed, and then a cluster analysis (sections 5.1 and 5.2). Moreover, a regression analysis was made of the sample data, in order to test certain hypotheses derived from the theory of innovative milieux. The presumption is that a multivariate factor analysis will produce relatively fewer factors for examination than are found in the data as a whole. These factors represent a set of many interrelated variables, selected to represent the structural characteristics and innovative behaviour of the sampled SMEs. The factor analysis was followed by a cluster analysis that puts homogeneous groups of sampled firms together in terms of the factors derived from the factor analysis. This statistical technique is used to classify the sampled firms according to their structural characteristics, performance and conduct.

Finally, the concluding section (5.3) discusses the similarities and discrepancies of the empirical realities in the West of England and Singapore-Johor agglomerations, and the 'model' put forward in the literature of innovative milieux, industrial districts and growth triangles. Both agglomerations represent examples of distinct, specialised, highly developed and complex systems. The comparative analysis yields further insights, and has implications for the identification of ways of facilitating and stimulating the innovative behaviour of less innovative SMEs in high-technology agglomerations.

5.1 A Statistical Analysis of the West of England Sample Survey

Factor analysis was performed on the whole of the West of England sample data. Consequently, through experimentation, and a process of elimination of the large number of variables, we can extract three principal factors from the data. Only variables appearing in each factor with the highest factor loading were taken into account. The analysis is presented in the Appendix, and its principal factors in Table 5.1.

Table 5.1: The Principal Factors of the West of England Data Survey

Factor 1	Factor 2	Factor 3
INN company patented an innovation		
REGR&DPT R&D department situated in the South West		
LEMPL size (log of number of employees)		
BRINN breakthrough innovation		
	COLSUP collaboration with suppliers	
	SKILSTAR recruitment of skilled staff from regional companies/organisations	
	SKILLED (-) % of employees designated as scientists/engineer or administrators/managers	
		REGCAFE (-) cafeteria effect (informal contact of managers)
		EMBED (-) regional embeddedness (work placements etc.)
Explained Variability (%)		
26	21	19

Source: Own survey.

From the statistical point of view, the results obtained from the factor analyses are satisfying. The first factor derived is named *INNOCO*, explaining 26% of total variance, and characterises larger innovative SMEs (in patents and breakthrough innovation) with a regional R&D department. The second factor, *SUPCHACO*, explaining 21% of sample variance, can be interpreted as a supply chain arrangement of firms. It shows that the sampled firms collaborate with their suppliers, and recruit their workforce primarily from other regional companies and institutions. However, the majority of their workforce is unskilled (hence the negative sign of the SKILLED variable), implying that they are firms involved in component manufacturing rather than in an R&D partnership. Finally, the third factor, *ISOLCO*, explains 19% of sample variance, and stresses the lack of a collective dimension for some companies. These rather small in size and innovative-averse companies are isolates. Their managers do not socialise with those of other regional or local companies from other sectors, and do not contribute to their local communities (hence the negative signs of their respective variables).

The next step in factor analysis is to employ a cluster analysis aiming at constructing groups of companies sharing the same characteristics. There is a choice here of selecting either the three principal factors identified in the cluster analysis or using the original variables. However, both analyses employed (shown in the Appendix) produce similar results to those shown in Figure 5.1. Nevertheless, it is worth stressing that factor and cluster analyses allow some discretion in the choice of variables and in defining the number of clusters.

From both cluster analyses, three almost identical clusters were identified. The first is composed of 23 firms presenting the following similarities:

(a) they collaborate with their suppliers;
(b) they employ (rather unskilled) staff, recruited from local companies;
(c) they are innovation-averse entities;
(d) they do not take advantage of collective learning; and
(e) they are of average size.

The second cluster is composed of 24 firms, which are:

(a) small in size;
(b) non-innovative; and
(c) non-collaborative.

The third cluster of 14 companies includes the *ideal types of company* postulated in the theoretical concept of innovative milieux examined in chapter 2. Firms share the following characteristics:

(a) they carry out high levels of innovation, including breakthrough innovations;
(b) they have a regionally based R&D department or facility;
(c) their managers display a high degree of socialisation with those from companies from other sectors;

(d) they are embedded in the local community; and
(e) they are large SMEs (larger than our sample mean of 80 employees).

Cluster analysis has made it possible to define how high-technology SMEs differentiate in terms of their innovative behaviour, structural characteristics and attitude towards collective and collaborating learning within the same sub-regional environment. Size appears to be a very important variable in determining the innovative behaviour of companies in the West of England. This assertion becomes evident by regressing the *INNOCO* factor with the size variable EMPL denoting number of employees (log of EMPL) (Table 5.2). This shows that the larger SMEs are more likely to be the regional innovators. The non-significant results of regression analyses of the other two factors also support this assertion. However, when we try to test the hypothesis that innovation in general, and breakthrough innovation in particular, are positively correlated with collective learning, the results are inconclusive. By regressing the *INNOCO* factor with the *REGCAFE* variable alone (a proxy of collective learning) no significant relationship is found. Although this variable (and that of collective learning) is not individually important for the innovative

Figure 5.1: Cluster Analysis of the West of England Data Survey

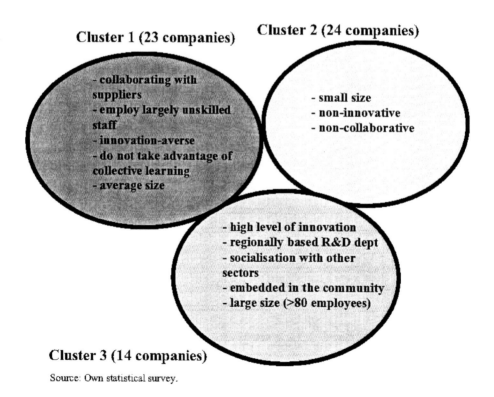

Cluster 1 (23 companies)

- collaborating with suppliers
- employ largely unskilled staff
- innovation-averse
- do not take advantage of collective learning
- average size

Cluster 2 (24 companies)

- small size
- non-innovative
- non-collaborative

- high level of innovation
- regionally based R&D dept
- socialisation with other sectors
- embedded in the community
- large size (>80 employees)

Cluster 3 (14 companies)

Source: Own statistical survey.

Table 5.2: Regression Analyses

Explanatory variables	*INNOCO*	*ISOLCO*
LEMPL	positive*	
REGCAFE		negative*
R-sq	52%	68%

*significant at 1%
Source: Statistical processing of own survey.

behaviour of the companies, collectively (with the LEMPL, INN, REGR&DPT, EMBED and BRINN variables) it is important, as is shown in the cluster analysis in Figure 5.1. In addition, by regressing the *ISOLCO* factor (which denotes innovation-averse behaviour) with the REGCAFE variable, we find the lack of collective learning or lack of socialisation to be statistically important for such isolators (hence the negative sign in Table 5.1).

From the preceding analyses, a clear picture of the innovative SME and its behaviour has begun to emerge. However, the comparison of the empirical case study of the West of England agglomeration with the ideal-type innovative milieu model presented in chapter 2 allows us to identify three important discrepancies:

* It is the medium-sized and not the small-sized SMEs that are radical innovators.
* Within high-technology clusters, the behaviour patterns of SMEs can be highly heterogeneous.
* Compared with the model of the innovative milieu, the West of England agglomeration is less co-operative and has developed rather limited associative relations that enhance innovativeness.

Nevertheless, the results of the above analysis indicate that, at least for the firms examined here, the West of England regional agglomeration is the principal site at which innovative SMEs learn to appropriate collective learning. The 'ideal' type of SME constitutes only a quarter of the total sample, however, suggesting that the task ahead for regional or local industrial policy-makers will be extremely challenging.

5.2 A Statistical Analysis of the Singapore-Johor Sample Survey

Factor analysis was also performed on the whole of the Singapore-Johor data. Again, three principal factors were extracted, in which only variables appearing in each factor with the highest factor loading were taken into account. The analysis is presented in the Appendix and its principal factors in Table 5.3. The analysis yields some important insights into the principal factors that influence high-technology SMEs in the agglomeration.

From the statistical point of view, the results obtained from the factor analysis of the Singapore-Johor data are adequate. The first factor is named *LOCSTART*, explaining 44% of total variance, and characterises regionally owned and knowledge-intensive firms which employ a skilled workforce, produce new products, are dependent on the

Table 5.3: The Principal Factors of the Singapore-Johor Data Survey

Factor 1	Factor 2	Factor 3
SKILL % of scientists/engineers and administrators/managers		
NEWPR % of sales of new product		
RAVSTF availability of research/engineering staff		
RQUSTF quality of research/engineering staff		
OWNMME owner/founder had managerial experience		
OWNRQ owner/founder had research/engineering qualifications		
	RSETUP set-up by other firm	
		RDI expenditure on R&D as % of sales
Explained Variability (%)		
44	**21**	**16**

Source: Own survey.

availability and quality of regional research/engineering staff, and have owners with research qualifications as well as managerial experience and qualifications. The second factor, *SETUPCO*, explaining 21% of sample variance, can be interpreted as a subsidiary firm which has been set up by another company displaying a very low innovative output and R&D intensity. It is possible that the factor represents a contract manufacturer or the regional headquarters of a foreign company. Finally, the third factor, *INDINNO*, explaining just 16% of sample variance, suggests a company that spends resources on R&D but is neither embedded in the regional economy nor is owned by a regional entrepreneur.

The next step in factor analysis is to employ the customary cluster analysis, aiming at constructing groups of firms sharing the same characteristics. Again, we have a choice here of selecting either the three principal factors identified in the cluster analysis or using the original variables. However, both analyses employed (shown in the Appendix) produce similar, albeit not identical, results. Figure 5.2 shows three groups of firms resulting from the cluster analysis using the principal factors derived from the factor analysis.

Figure 5.2: Cluster Analysis of the Singapore-Johor Data Survey

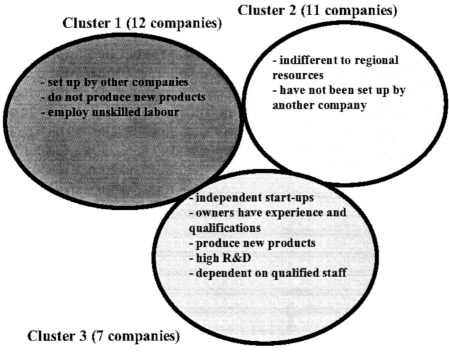

Cluster 2 (11 companies)

Cluster 1 (12 companies)

- set up by other companies
- do not produce new products
- employ unskilled labour

- indifferent to regional resources
- have not been set up by another company

- independent start-ups
- owners have experience and qualifications
- produce new products
- high R&D
- dependent on qualified staff

Cluster 3 (7 companies)

Source: Own statistical survey.

From both cluster analyses, three almost identical clusters were identified. The first is the largest, composed of 12 innovation-averse subsidiaries presenting the following similarities:

(a) they have been set up by other companies;
(b) they do not produce any significant number of new products; and
(c) they employ unskilled labour.

The second cluster comprises 11 innovation-averse indigenous firms which:

(a) are indifferent to regional resources, such as the availability and quality of researchers/engineers and managers; and
(b) have not been set up by another company.

The third cluster consists of the remaining 7 firms, which are characterised by the following:

Table 5.4: Regression Analyses

Explanatory variable	LOCSTART	SETUPCO	INDINNO
OWNRQ	positive*	negative	positive
R-sq	60%	14%	0%

*significant at 1%
Source: Statistical processing of own survey.

(a) they are independent start-ups in which their owners have research and managerial qualifications, and managerial experience;

(b) they produce new products, employ skilled workforce, and have high R&D intensity; and

(c) they are dependent on the agglomeration's qualified staff.

The companies in the third cluster are perhaps the 'ideal' type of innovative firm. They are indigenous companies managed by an experienced and qualified entrepreneur who is taking advantage of the collective learning and economic complementarities of the Singapore-Johor agglomeration. Some of these firms display a clear division of labour, having their manufacturing operations in Johor (mainly involved with contract and/or assembly works) and their headquarters and R&D activities in Singapore. However, it is important to note that this is a substantial group, representing one third of the sampled firms. It is a dynamic cluster of innovative SMEs, which constantly develop their technological capacity.

Cluster analysis has made it possible to identify how SMEs within the same sub-regional environment of Singapore-Johor differentiate in terms of innovative behaviour and ownership. The research/engineering or managerial experience and qualifications of the entrepreneur himself appear to be an important variable in determining the innovative trajectory of firms in the agglomeration. This assertion is validated by regressing the *LOCSTART* derived factor on the OWNRQ factor, denoting entrepreneurial expertise, or so-called *technopreneurship*[1]. The regression results indicate that indigenous firms created by people with research/engineering qualifications are more likely to be successful innovators. The non-significant results of regression analyses of the other derived structural factors (i.e. *SETUPCO*, denoting a contract/assembly manufacturing type of firm, and *INDINNO*, denoting an independent firm) also support this assertion.

To conclude, the comparison of the ideal type of innovative milieu in the case study of the Singapore-Johor agglomeration allows us to make the following remarks:

* In the Singapore-Johor agglomeration it is the indigenous SMEs, rather than TNCs' subsidiaries, which are (radical) innovators
* Within high-technology clusters, innovative SMEs are a minority
* Innovators take advantage of the regional resources and economic complementarities of the agglomeration

* Policy-makers need to encourage the development of indigenous SMEs and promote entrepreneurship

5.3. Industrial Districts, Innovative Milieux, Growth Triangles or Global Knowledge Economies?

This section concludes by returning to the concepts of industrial districts and innovative milieux, and to the identification of ways of facilitating and stimulating the innovative behaviour of all regional SMEs. It is important to compare the two empirical cases and identify similarities and differences with the innovative milieu model. We have already identified some of the differences in the preceding sections. It is appropriate now to collect all the available information and consider whether both agglomerations match the ideal of the innovative milieu. Such information includes not only the sample survey, but also the data collected from in-depth interviews with experts, decision-makers and secondary sources.

With respect to the comparison between the West of England agglomeration and the innovative milieu model, the available evidence suggests a pattern of uneven innovation trajectory. Although the agglomeration in general has achieved a specialisation in precision engineering, electronics, communication and computer services, its north-eastern part, namely the Cheltenham-Gloucester urban area of the county of Gloucestershire, is experiencing a regional diversification of its sectoral structure. This area is evolving away from its traditional specialisation in defence/aerospace towards automobile components and medical health care technologies. The important regional collective actors operating in the county are the Training and Enterprise Council, Business Link, Gloucestershire Development Agency, and the County Council. The county has a good reputation for being innovative, and a culture of innovation exists in its high-technology, precision-engineering sector. As in the rest of the West of England, the county has a highly qualified and skilled labour force. It also benefits from being close to Oxford, an important knowledge centre and cluster of high technology in the UK. There is also a trend in this area towards the development of supply chains, especially within the Western Aerospace Forum. However, local firms place more emphasis on competition than collaboration.

The empirical investigation identified a small number of spin-offs in the Cheltenham-Gloucester area from large regional companies, such as Dayford Designs and Racal Services, as well as from European and American multinationals. Also, some anecdotal evidence indicates that there are other spin-offs, originating from Dowty, Smiths, Rank Xerox, Renishaw, and Walls. However, the findings from the Cheltenham-Gloucester area indicate that the intensity and quality of collaboration among the local SMEs is lower than in the rest of the West of England. The majority of smaller SMEs are crisis-driven and reactive, rather than proactive learning organisations. They are more likely to be involved with information gathering than with knowledge acquisition or competence consolidation and development. All this suggests that the area is an industrial district rather than an innovative milieu.

However, the southern part of Gloucestershire (the area around the towns of Stroud

Table 5.5: Main Characteristics of Small Innovative and Knowledge-intensive Firms in the West of England and Singapore-Johor Agglomerations

Dimensions	West of England N 61	Singapore-Johor N 30
Ranking of main sectors in which sampled firms belong	1. Engineering 2. Electronics and Telecommunications 3. Computer Services 4. Medical Equipment	1. Electronics and Telecommunications 2. Engineering 3. Electronic Services 4. Contract Manufacturing in Electronics/Electrical goods
R&D spending as % of sales (averages)	6.3%	9.8%
% of firms with patented innovations	34%	23%
Number of breakthrough innovations (%)	10 (16%)	6 (20%)
% of skilled workforce	63%	32%
% of customers contributing to firms' innovation process	39%	73%
Frequency of informal contacts of managers with other regional managers	Moderate	High
New local start-ups by former employees (%)	36%	50%
% of *'ideal'* type of firms, and their attributes (derived by employing cluster and factor analyses on the sample data)	25% • High level of innovation • A regionally based R&D facility • Large degree of socialisation of managers • Larger companies (>80 employees)	23% • Independent start-ups • Owners/founders have both research/engineering and managerial experience and qualifications • Produce new products, employ skilled workforce, and have high R&D intensity • Dependence on the agglomeration's qualified staff

Source: Konstadakopulos, 2001.

and Cirencester) together with the rest of the West of England (from the Bristol-Bath urban agglomeration to Swindon) is possibly approximating to an innovative milieu. In this area, our survey results reveal that production of external economies is quite high, contributing to the efficiency and growth of the sub-regional agglomeration. During the last two decades, the area has seen a significant growth of innovative SMEs due to the presence of a large number of local technology-based companies and a plethora of research and support institutions. The most important finding is the fact that over a third of sampled firms have patented an innovation, and more than one fifth have produced a breakthrough innovation, taking on board and benefiting from regional collective learning. At the same time, some intra-regional diffusion of technological expertise is taking place, as 39% of innovative SMEs' managers previously worked for a regional firm. However, this does not compare favourably with the Cambridge agglomeration, in which 81% of technology-based SMEs' founders come from the locality (Keeble et al., 1999, p. 324). Nevertheless, interviews with local firms suggest that there are some important regional advantages in the West of England. Company managers commented that *'there are high-tech resources in the area'*, *'it is a creative environment'*, *'there is a centre of excellence in this region'*, *'we get IT graduates from local universities'*, and so on. Moreover, some regional universities are starting to play a more proactive role, especially in graduate research recruitment and in creating a constructive co-operative mode of interaction with local companies. The Teaching Company Scheme, for example, allows research students to work in a company on a research project which is supervised by a university. It must also be emphasised that the West of England firms have recently developed close relations and collaboration with their customers and suppliers in response to intensifying competition - a direct result of the processes of European integration and globalisation.

Moving to the Singapore-Johor agglomeration, a close examination of the structural characteristics of the sampled firms reveals that their operations are part of a two-tier division of labour. Because of spatial complementarities, R&D and manufacturing in the electronics and electrical and precision engineering sectors are two key tasks undertaken in Singapore, while contract and/or assembly manufacturing is the main task undertaken in Johor. In addition, the division of labour among contract and assembly firms in Johor is low, and contrasts with the model of the innovative milieu. However, the local production system in the state capital, Johor Bahru, is part of the much larger cross-border production system of the SIJORI growth triangle. In the last two decades, the Singapore-Johor agglomeration has gradually changed and evolved. The area has seen the creation of new high-technology firms and has acquired a specialisation in electronics, engineering and electrical goods that has led to an increase in output and exports, and improvement in quality. There is little doubt that the agglomeration - the core of the growth triangle - has now become one of the leading high-technology clusters in the ASEAN region, possibly approximating to an innovative milieu.

The survey results indicate that collective learning is taking place in this cross-border agglomeration. It has witnessed a significant growth of indigenous innovative SMEs that have been acquiring know-how from the large number of technology-based TNCs and from a network of over fifteen research institutes and research centres. The sampled SMEs spend a relatively large proportion of their revenues (9.8%) on R&D, a quarter of them have patented an innovation, and most importantly one fifth have produced breakthrough innovations. In Singapore, public support for innovation in the form of innovation grants[2] has been instrumental in raising the innovativeness of the area. It is these innovative firms which are taking advantage of, and benefiting from, the regional collective learning of the Singapore-Johor area.

At the same time, intra-regional diffusion of technological expertise is clearly taking place in the Singapore-Johor milieu, given the fact that two thirds of skilled staff of the sampled innovative SMEs were previously employed in another regional firm. It is the mobility of the above skilled scientists, engineers and top managers, carrying with them an accumulated technological expertise and knowledge that sustains the innovative capability of the area. However, the locational advantages of the Singapore-Johor agglomeration are equally important. It is acknowledged that proximity and spatial density of firms in metropolitan areas facilitates the diffusion of information on technology and business conditions (Antonelli, 2000, p. 542). The majority of managers interviewed for the present study commented on the importance of Singapore's locational advantages for their company's performance, and put forward the following inter-linked attributing factors: the strategic locational advantage of Singapore as a regional hub; the availability of a highly skilled workforce; the presence of excellent infrastructure; the good business reputation of the area; the stable political system; and the pro-business attitude of the government. Other managers highlighted the importance of high-tech TNCs, and the R&D potential of the area. Managers in Johor stressed the importance of proximity to Singapore and the benefits of clustering, pointing out that the most important of their customers are now located in the Singapore-Johor area. However, there are a few disadvantages in being located in Singapore and/or Johor. Company managers complained about the rise of labour and other fixed costs, as well as the small size of the Singaporean market. For companies located in Johor, the main disadvantage was rising production costs, given the fact that the State of Johor is considered to have higher living costs than any other Malaysian state. An additional disadvantage was the underdeveloped infrastructure network (including Internet connections), and the lack of an organised business information and support system.

It is important to mention here that the sampled firms exhibit high levels of interaction with companies (suppliers or customers) situated outside their milieu (i.e. in the rest of Malaysia, Japan, Europe and the US). Many of these companies tap into national and international innovation (and other) networks, which are providing them with the knowledge and know-how to become world-class innovators. As a result, we observe an increase in the capacity of firms to innovate and bring new products, processes and knowledge to the global market place. The same is true for the sampled firms in the West of England. They ranked other UK regions beyond the South West as the most common location of their collaborators, followed jointly by Europe and the South West of England.

These findings support the view that both regional agglomerations are simultaneously knowledge-based and globalised, allowing input to the current debate on the so-called new economy and on globalisation. Firstly, in both agglomerations we discern a trend towards globalisation of innovation in the context of the knowledge-based economy. Secondly, we find strong evidence that geographical proximity and the institutional setting play an instrumental role in determining the learning capability and innovative behaviour of high-technology SMEs. At least for the firms examined here, regional agglomerations remain the principal area within which firms interact with each other and engage in collective learning. In the West of England it is mostly the indigenous firms that have a regionally based R&D facility, displaying high levels of innovation. In Singapore-Johor it is again largely the indigenous firms, rather than the subsidiaries of multinational companies, who are the major innovators. Moreover, regional links and regional resources are very important to them. It appears, therefore, that the findings echo those of Gertler et al. (2000, p. 688), who compared the innovative behaviour of manufacturing firms in Ontario, Canada. They noted that indigenous firms were 'more likely to perform innovative activities locally and are more embedded in the Ontario economy than their multinational counterparts'.

Despite the fact that both the West of England and the Singapore-Johor agglomerations approximate to an innovative milieu, the current empirical investigation has identified some important differences concerning the intensity, frequency and quality of interaction among firms (Table 5.5). The first of these is the well-developed synergy and sociability experienced by the sampled SMEs in the Singapore-Johor agglomeration, compared with the rather individualistic attitude of SMEs in the West of England. For instance, in Singapore-Johor, 73% of firms said that their customers had contributed to the firm's innovation process, while in the West of England only 39% of firms reported that this was the case. Moreover, the frequency of informal socialisation of firms' managers with those from other sectors is much higher in the Singapore-Johor agglomeration. Therefore, learning to innovate is a more intense collective process - external to each firm, and yet internal to the agglomeration - in Singapore-Johor than in the West of England.

The second important difference is that the high-technology SMEs in the West of England employed twice as many skilled workers as similar firms in Singapore-Johor. A skilled workforce generates a stronger effect of collective learning, and this is reflected in the greater number of firms in the West of England with patented innovations, in comparison with Singapore-Johor. However, the latter exhibits a higher percentage of new local start-ups by the firms' former employees, and this can weaken collective learning (Table 5.5).

It is a distinct possibility that these differences of collective efficiency between the innovative milieux of the West of England and Singapore-Johor may be due to external factors. The West of England milieu is more mature[3] and developed than its counterpart, but this doesn't wholly explain the difference; some of the afore-mentioned external factors are also major determinants. Locke draws attention to the importance of the social development of Milan, contrasting its culture with that of Turin. He claims that what distinguishes Milan from Turin is 'highly qualitative attributes like the 'openness' or 'parochialism' of particular interest groups and the kinds of linkages (strong vs. weak) that exist among the various local actors' (1995, pp. 122-3). In a similar way, Kanter highlights the importance of social infrastructure, or what she calls the infrastructure for collaboration, necessary for global success. This consists of 'networks among small and large companies in related industries, between suppliers and customers, between ethnic groups and neighbourhoods, or among institutions in a community that contribute to quality of life' (Kanter, 1995, pp. 362-363). It is to a discussion of these economic, political and social determinants that we turn in the next and final chapter.

Notes

[1] The Singaporean government has been active in promoting technopreneurship (technology entrepreneurs). In 1999, it invested US$1 billion in a technopreneurship investment fund. However, it is open to question whether exceptionally talented investor-businessmen can be created through state intervention (Low, 2001, p. 423). See also the discussion in the final chapter on the necessary political and regulatory changes that have to be made to create such technopreneurs.

[2] For instance, between 1996 and 1999 the EDB in Singapore made 480 innovation grants, mostly to indigenous companies (*The Sunday* [Singapore] *Times*, 2 May 1999). However, Singapore has not been able to substantially increase the technological output of its indigenous firms, as have some of their Asian competitors. Statistics from the World Bank indicate that 'Singaporean companies registered only 311 patents in 1998, compared with 50,714 registered by Korean companies during the same period - a vast difference, even when population disparity is taken into account' (Konstadakopulos, 2002, p. 106).

[3] For instance, the average age of sampled firms in the West of England is 16 years, compared with 10 years in Singapore-Johor.

Part III: Policy Lessons and Implications

Chapter 6:

The Relevance of the Economic, Political and Social Environments of Europe and South-East Asia

It is apparent that there are considerable differences between the West of England and Singapore-Johor high-technology agglomerations with regard to collective efficiency, innovativeness and levels of development. Contrasting technological policies, and economic, political and social processes based on strong historical legacies, have also shaped the two innovative milieux. On the other hand, as shown by the analysis, various common external pressures are starting to affect their evolution. The process of globalisation of innovation in the emerging knowledge-based economy is one of the most significant of these pressures, and is undoubtedly influencing the development of regional high-technology agglomerations.

However, this process is, to paraphrase Giddens (1999), a phenomenon that is not just technological but also economic, political, and cultural. It is acknowledged that globalisation reduces the significance of local space as the primary location for innovation, as firms now have access to innovations on a global basis (Vellinga, 2000; Yeoh et al., 2001; Debrah et al., 2002). Globalisation therefore encourages inter- and intra-regional collaboration, and enhances the spread of trans-border practices (Higgott, 1999, p. 92; Breslin and Higgott, 2000, p. 344). This means, of course, that the erosion of economic and political boundaries in Europe and in ASEAN has influenced the innovative milieux of the West of England and Singapore-Johor, and the social relations and business activities of their respective agglomerations. Moreover, as we have seen in the previous chapters, the liberalisation of trade has led to an extensive network of inter-firm co-operation, extending to firms situated in other regions and trading blocs.

In this chapter, we look at the relevance of the broad economic, political and social environments that influence the learning behaviour of knowledge-intensive SMEs in their respective milieux. This topic touches on some of the issues that were dealt with in chapters 1 and 2. There we discussed some theoretical aspects of the innovative milieu, and described the evolution of technological policies in both Europe and South-East Asia. It is in looking at the influence of the wider socio-political and socio-economic environment on the innovative milieu in which the firm operates that we

101

begin to see how far that environment is shaping the overall innovation performance of the regional agglomeration. Such examination will allow us to draw policy implications, based on the empirical findings that transcend the constraints of the firm.

The present chapter begins by looking at market cultures in Europe and South-East Asia, and in particular at how such cultures influence the learning capability, innovative activity and sociability of firms. It then turns to a discussion of the two competing models of technological development. The third section of the chapter focuses on policy lessons and implications, while the final section attempts to make some practical recommendations.

6.1 Market Cultures in the Economies of Europe and South-East Asia

In this section it is argued that the extraordinary growth of both the West of England and Singapore-Johor agglomerations can be characterised more accurately as a form of 'business-led' development. The main influences behind the agglomerations' technological advancement are not only the national or regional governments (or even supranational institutions), and government-linked corporations, but also the owners of indigenous, high-technology SMEs and managers of TNCs operating outside the control of national governments. The economic dynamics, innovativeness and organisation of both agglomerations can be best understood in the wider context of social relationships among firms, and between firms and business support institutions, as well as intercultural communication and transnational networks. It is the social and organisational structure of both agglomerations that constructs a 'market culture' in which economic decisions and activities, including the adoption of new technologies, are taking place. Indeed, Thrift talks about a 'new' market culture, an outcome of the new economy, in which 'technology could be constantly modulated and so constantly redefined - to the advantage of many stakeholders' (Thrift, 2001, p. 429).

Here we attempt to analyse market processes that may influence the innovative behaviour of firms, in relation to their cultural and organisational backgrounds. Firstly, we discard the simplistic view that depicts European and South-East Asian cultures as being homogenous. Both Europe and South-East Asia are remarkably culturally diverse and complex regions. Secondly, we adopt the assumption made in recent cultural studies which presumes that the cultural dimensions of economic activity are no more influential than politics or economics in shaping recent market development (Hefner, 1998, p. 5; Werbner, 1999, p. 549). Thirdly, we assert that in the West of England and Singapore-Johor, market cultures have been influenced by the areas' unique characteristics. Thus, the social relations and vibrant market cultures of the agglomerations are intrinsic to national, regional or even supranational politics, and to ideology (Vellinga, 2000, p. 306). From this perspective, in examining market cultures we shall consider some factors that affect the business environment in our two agglomerations. These factors influence both national/regional policies and, by extension, the decision-making of individual firms.

In a previous publication (Konstadakopulos, 2001), the author identified a number of such factors:

(i) The process of regional integration that is taking place within the EU (i.e. economic and monetary union) and ASEAN (i.e. the creation of a Free Trade Area (AFTA)). Both redefine the cultural, social, political and economic bonds of their members and their firms.

(ii) The process of rapid technological and social changes (such as greater participation of women or immigrants in employment) affecting the agglomerations' industrial structure and competitiveness.

(iii) The increase in the economic dependency of regional economies. As explained in chapter 2, the extent of economic complementarities in the Singapore-Johor cross-border area is exceptionally high. The regional economy of the South West of England is similarly dependent on the rest of Britain and Europe for its market outputs.

(iv) The liberal democracy of European space, and the so-called 'soft' authoritarianism adopted by the political systems of Singapore and Malaysia, encourage the growth of private ownership and a consumerist society. The governing parties in these two South-East Asian countries, the Political Action Party (PAP) in Singapore and the United Malays National Organisation (UMNO) in Malaysia[1], have governed their respective countries since the 1960s, and dominate social and economic life. This dominance has affected cultural proclivities.

As argued in chapter 2, the emerging knowledge-based economy is currently restructuring the economies of both regional agglomerations. We have also sketched the background to the development of technological policies in both areas. If we are to fully comprehend these policies, we need to understand the underlying logic and the socio-political processes in which they are embedded. What, essentially, is the motivation behind the policies? Which of the following factors are the most influential?

* a historically strong regional specialisation
* socio-political embeddedness
* effective information and knowledge networks
* existence of knowledge institutions, or
* strong local and/or regional culture

An investigation by the author of the patterns of associationalism in the South West of England (Konstadakopulos, 2000a) - patterns which are confirmed by the survey data presented in chapter 3 - reveals a rather limited number of co-operative networks among economic actors such as companies and research institutions. The absence of strong associative order is attributed to the region's weak regional identity - the exception being the far South West, i.e. Cornwall. Inter-group relations among companies have been mostly adversarial, based on the Anglo-Saxon individualistic form of market culture as described by Hofstede (1980) and Calori (1994), rather than on co-operative spirit. This form of market culture is characterised by a high level of liberalism, individualism and profit orientation, extensive mobility of the skilled workforce, and modest R&D spending. As shown in chapters 4 and 5, these patterns of associationalism contrast with the characteristics of sociability or communitarian spirit, organised competition, intervention by government, and high investment in R&D spending observed in the Singapore-Johor cross-border area.

Despite economic competition and overlapping areas of economic interest, co-operation across the national boundaries of Singapore and Malaysia is relatively unproblematic, because the cultural gap between the two countries, which were formerly united (albeit for a short period), is relatively insignificant. The educational system, the media, popular culture and the wide use of English language in business transactions all provide potential common grounds. In addition, as we shall see in the next section, the official rhetoric in both countries continuously stresses the common so-called *Asian values* that unite them. The concern, if not obsession, with these values is important here, as it links Chinese, Malay and Indian business cultures within the model of Asian capitalism, as distinct from the 'western' model. Must we therefore make an analytical distinction between two different market cultures - one European, the other South-East Asian - and, by implication, two competing models of economic development? The answer to this question goes to the heart of the debate on Asian values. It has been argued these values shaped market cultures in the past, but can they continue to do so in future? Some of our interviewees echoed international commentators in raising questions about the extent of Asian values, and their validity, arguing that the concept has now run its course.

Nonetheless, our findings highlight the importance of informal social links and knowledge sharing as sources for firms' innovation. Dense knowledge-sharing networks are created, which show a tendency to cluster in regional and urban agglomerations. Globalisation, therefore, is creating new innovative milieux around knowledge-intensive industries. This conforms to the so-called *glocalisation* process described in the globalisation literature, which postulates that innovation and knowledge have become localised, while trade and capital markets have been globalised (Leadbeater, 1999; Olds et al., 1999; Beck, 2000; Jessop and Sum, 2000).

A central feature of the technologically advanced and innovative milieu of the West of England is its distinctive specialisation in defence/aerospace, electronics, telecommunications, and the multimedia industry. Another is its endogenous type of growth. Its market culture, a model of independent capitalism (Calori et al., 1994, p. 32), breeds a fair number of creative and entrepreneurial knowledge workers. A new type of enterprise is emerging in the knowledge-driven sectors of this sub-region that produces, utilises, disseminates and adds value to knowledge rather than manufactures goods. At the same time, the process of globalisation and the emergence of e-commerce are obliging regional high-technology SMEs to take notice of markets beyond their British and even European context. The South West of England, through its Regional Development Agency, has started to evolve a strategic technology policy that is encouraging collective and collaborative learning among regional firms. However, Britain's reluctance to take part in European Monetary Union is seen as a significant disadvantage, because potential high-technology investors might avoid the region, and invest instead in one of the regions of the euro-12 area.

The success of the Singapore-Johor hub of knowledge-driven industries, in particular in electronics, chemicals and precision engineering, is mainly the outcome of exogenous growth induced by foreign direct investment and stimulated by the activities of multinational companies from the mid-1980s to the mid-90s. The transfer of technology from TNCs to local firms, including SMEs, has been very important for the technological development of the Singapore-Johor agglomeration. However, it appears that only Singapore has been successful in forming technological alliances between TNCs and some of its indigenous firms, making the country an attractive location for R&D facilities. Johor, despite substantial government expenditure on physical infrastructure to facilitate R&D, is only a moderately attractive location. Without effective transfer of technology from TNCs, neither Singapore nor Malaysia would be able to move up the *technological ladder* mentioned in chapter 2.

Nevertheless, the agglomeration has been a technological adopter, and is perhaps becoming a world-class innovator and knowledge centre. Its success is partly due to South-East Asia's market culture, a model of dependent capitalism, which has achieved high economic growth with the help of a prescriptive social development, and top-down, authoritarian, government-led policies. There was some justification for such policies in the immediate post-colonial period, when the emerging plural societies and associated ethnic divisions of labour in Singapore and Malaysia were the source of major racial conflicts. In both countries, the politics of ethnicity[2] have played an important role in shaping their political economy and market cultures. In Malaysia, the ethnic divide, as well as antagonistic relations between the Malay government and Chinese- or Indian-dominated business, fuelled by the so-called New Economic Policy, have created openness to foreign capital. In Singapore, the government-led regionalisation policy has actively encouraged indigenous companies and foreign TNCs to move their labour-intensive and lower-skilled industries to Johor, and to the Riau islands in Indonesia. Singapore's multiracial business society, and particularly its large Chinese business community, is well-placed to cross the cultural gap separating it from its neighbours.

Singapore, therefore, is playing a central role in the development of a market culture in South-East Asia, as it has been able to transfer some of its business practices and its unique cultural and political values to its immediate ASEAN partners. The fluidity and informality of intercultural communication between the Chinese, Malaysian and Indian business elites has immensely helped the development of the Singapore-Johor agglomeration. More importantly, Singapore is seen as an archetypal *market state* (Koh, 1998), or *developmental state* (Low, 2001), offering to its ASEAN partners a regional model of social organisation, economic planning and economic growth. However, South-East Asia's market culture might have to rely on economic, social and even political change in order to produce the creative, innovative and skilled workforce needed for the global knowledge-based economy. A number of commentators suggest that the region must carry out substantial reforms in order to counter competition from China, which, since the mid-1990s, has received nearly four fifths of the foreign direct investment in Asia (a development that is not only slowing down South-East Asia's recovery, but also taking away the much-needed technological know-how and foreign skilled labour (*The Economist*, 17 March 2001; Freeman, 2001; Freeman and Hew, 2002; Konstadakopulos, 2002)). The first and most important reform to be made, according to *The Economist*, is a shift to sound democratic governance, coupled with transparency[3] and legal predictability. The second is the lowering of trade barriers within the framework of the non-materialised AFTA, and the last is the continuation of liberalisation of South-East Asia's regulated domestic capital markets, an important pre-condition for the return of international investors. These suggested reforms highlight the importance of the relationship between technology and knowledge acquisition, globalisation, and democracy. As Hay and Watson (1999) suggest, there is a definite trend towards globalisation of democracy, as opposed to the democratisation of globalisation, which is still a long way off. Although some South-East Asian countries have become more democratic, the rest need to follow in order to increase the region's prosperity.

A major influence that is forcing the pace of change in all regional agglomerations is undoubtedly information technology and the Internet. However, as Seely Brown and Duguid suggest, predictions on the so-called 'death of distance' and the dispersion of high-technology agglomerations due to the application of information technology have been premature (2000, p. 169). They point out that Silicon Valley, the heart of the information industry, continues to flourish. Although information technology and the Internet are bringing down geographical barriers, agglomeration economies in intangibles, such as skilled labour, accumulated tacit knowledge, collective learning, and research institutions, are still clustered in a small number of regions rather than dispersed worldwide (Kirat and Lung, 1999; Matthiessen et al., 2002). Many commentators believe that a number of social, political and cultural factors are influencing the transition of these agglomeration economies towards being knowledge-based (Hudson, 1999; Goh, 1999; Low, 2001; Lever, 2002). This also raises the question of which model of development is the most appropriate for all agglomerations and their firms. In the next section we look at two of the most important models, within the context of these factors.

6.1.1 Competing Models of Development

Within the recent theoretical literature on economic development, the prevailing view is that the classical endogenous factors of production - namely capital, land and labour - are inadequate for the competitiveness of an economic system. At the end of the 20th century, more and more commentators were highlighting the importance of a new type of economy based on a decisive production factor, i.e. knowledge. One of their central propositions was that knowledge and the process of learning would play a key role in the development of Europe, South-East Asia and the rest of the world in the 21st century.

Kuklinski (2000b, pp. 141-148) presents a compelling argument on the importance of knowledge for economic development. In his discussion relating to the future of Europe in the 21st century, in the context of global change, he articulates four dilemmas and puts forward five intuitive models or scenarios of development: the

Welfare, Darwinian, Thurovian, Singapurian and *Christian* models, incorporating innovation, knowledge production and economic growth. Two of these - the *Thurovian* and *Singapurian* - are considered to be the most pragmatic scenarios for the future, in global terms.

The *Thurovian model* is named after MIT economist Lester C. Thurow. In his celebrated book, *The Future of Capitalism*, Thurow comments that economic success will in future depend on investment in skills, education, knowledge and infrastructure (1996, p. 326), and in his later book, *Building Wealth* (1999), presents a detailed plan as to how individuals, firms and nations can and must build wealth in a knowledge-based global economy. According to Kuklinski, the Thurovian model is the most suitable for Europe. The main reason for this is that the involvement of the European Union in supporting the continent's knowledge-driven industries, which came about as a result of Europe's forty-year process of integration, is leading to the adoption of policies that Thurow claims are requisites for economic success (Kuklinski, 2000b, p. 145). Europe plays an important role in the creation of new knowledge in precision engineering, telecommunications, pharmaceuticals and high-valued services. Although it has a comparative advantage in skills, education and knowledge, it is lagging behind its main competitors, namely the United States and Japan, when it comes to the creation of wealth (Thurow, 1999, p. 86). However, since the mid-1990s the European Union has shifted towards a systemic and problem-orientated policy on research, innovation and training (Caracostas and Muldur, 2000, p. 16).

The European Commission in particular has taken a number of initiatives to expedite the shift towards a knowledge-based economy and society (as the Commission now refers to the concept, reflecting its desire to include the social dimension). Specifically, the White Paper on education and training (*Teaching and learning. Towards the learning society*, 1995) contains proposals for improving education and training. The Commission also set up a number of European networks, firstly under the COMETT and ERASMUS programmes, and secondly under SOCRATES and LEONARDO, which improved the transnational mobility of young people, students, teachers, researchers and trainers. The Green Paper on innovation (1995) and its successor, the *Action Plan for Innovation* (1996), have been instrumental in initiating a Europe-wide debate on the issues of innovation. Since 1984, the EU has also supported research in the form of five framework programmes. The fifth programme (1998-2002) has a budget of 15 billion, and supports four 'thematic' activities aimed at sustainable growth and the development of an information-based European economy and society. These are complemented by three 'horizontal' activities aimed at the globalisation of the EU's research, the promotion of innovation and participation of SMEs, and the improvement of human potential and the socio-economic knowledge-base. Many activities for the promotion of the knowledge-based economy and society have been incorporated in the Commission's 6th Framework Programme (2002-06) on the creation of a *'European Research Area'*.

In 1997, the European Union adopted a communication document entitled *Towards a Europe of Knowledge*, which acknowledges that there is a need to create a European common response to the challenges of the emerging knowledge-based economy, and sets out the guidelines for future actions. Finally, in 2000, the discussion document *Employment, Economic Reforms and Social Cohesion - Towards a Europe Based on Innovation and Knowledge* highlighted the need for Europe to hasten her transition to a knowledge-based economy by investing in human resources.

However, nurturing a knowledge-based economy and society is a formidable challenge, and there is no guarantee that Europe will be able to make the necessary economic, political and social changes to take advantage of its educated and skilled human capital. Kuklinski suggests that the only alternative solution for Europe, and in particular central and eastern Europe, is to adopt the so-called *Singapurian model* of development (2000b, p. 145), which is based on a high degree of order that has produced unprecedented wealth.

Kuklinski thinks highly of the *Singapurian model* (which is also applicable to Malaysia)[4]. He agrees that the political system of Singapore limits individual freedom as a trade-off for improved collective order and growing economic efficiency, and that the model is 'a great contradiction to the fundamental values of the European culture and civilization'. Nevertheless, the *Singapurian model* has been so successful that it needs to be taken seriously (Kuklinski, 2000b, p. 145). Thurow also praises the extraordinary success of Singapore, and compares it with Israel - another small country, but one which is based on individual ingenuity rather than collective order, and has consequently had only moderate success (1999, pp. 104-105).

In many ways, Singapore and Malaysia exemplify both the accomplishment and the weakness of the economic model that brought about the so-called *Asian economic miracle*. During the last three decades, both countries have created consistent prosperity in the form of better education, housing and health care, improved infrastructure, more consumer goods and more leisure. But such prosperity brings with it major drawbacks - social inequality, a highly commercialised attitude, cultural bewilderment, environmental degradation, and political insecurity, not to mention recessions and financial crises. The major economic and social problems of South-East Asia are well known. They are clearly described in the *The Trouble with Tigers - The Rise and Fall of South-East Asia*, by the *Financial Times* journalist Victor Mallet (1999). The author agrees that South-East Asia has been economically successful, but argues that its citizens have been burdened with many costs in relation to their political, social and cultural environments. Haley and Low also point out that Singaporean citizens have now become 'depoliticized, docile and consumerist' (1998, p. 531). It is also the case that Malays have been subject, for some time now, to a corrupt political system and extreme racial tensions (Clad, 1989; Schlossstein, 1991; *The Economist*, 12 February 2000; Chin, 2000).

Undoubtedly, political authoritarianism in Singapore and Malaysia has created the macroeconomic stability that has underpinned the rapid economic growth. Moreover, the pro-business leadership in both countries has provided the appropriate institutional framework for the promotion of innovation and technological development. Since Singapore's independence in 1965, and following its departure from the short-lived Malay Federation, former Prime Minister Lee Kuan Yew's PAP has controlled Singapore's political and economic life. The architect of Singapore's success,

Lee Kuan Yew - who is now Senior Minister, having handed over the Prime Minister's post to Goh Chock Tong in 1990 - has replaced political turmoil with 'an extraordinary depoliticization of public life' (Hamilton-Hart, 2000, p. 195). Despite the absence of western-type politics and interest-group constraints, Singapore's governing system is competent, efficient and honest, and is much admired by its business community. However, it is important to mention that the majority of the sampled firms in Singapore praised the pro-business administration, as well as the pragmatism and flexibility of government departments in controlling economic development and promotion of learning for innovation.

More importantly, Singapore's governing elite has a reputation for being practically corruption-free, while potential for social unrest is now extremely low. Some observers take the simplistic view that such social stability is reinforced by Confucius's teachings on the values of good human interrelations, discipline, thrift, and hard labour, while others find Confucian values[5] in South-East Asia to be largely irrelevant (Mackie, 1998, p. 134; Vines, 1999, pp. 75-76). Hamilton-Hart, in her comprehensive review of the Singaporean state, argues that its record of efficient and clean government is based on formal government and informal institutions being closely linked to private interests. However, pervasive ties between the government and the business elite could in future make the system of government fragile and prone to corruption (2000, pp. 195-216).

Since the creation of Malaysia in 1965, following the brief unsuccessful merger with Singapore, UMNO and its coalition partners have controlled the federation's political system. Dr Mahathir Mohamad, a popular leader and skilful politician, has been Prime Minister for the last twenty years. In December 1999 he led his ruling coalition to a hasty election, in which he managed to retain his two-thirds majority. However, he is now faced with opposition parties united by his dismissal and prosecution of Anwar Ibrahim, his former deputy and finance minister.

Although Lee Kuan Yew and Dr Mahathir have been fierce antagonists, they have both been advocates of *Asian values*. They point out that Asians are different from westerners in specific elements of culture, e.g. emphasis on personal thrift, hard work, self-discipline, and greater respect for education, family, community and government (Mallet, 1999, p. 7). Thurow points out that countries like Singapore and Taiwan have benefited from values such as personal thrift by using the higher than average savings made by their citizens to build semiconductor foundries and become world leaders in semiconductor chip production (Thurow, 1999, p. 56). However, Haley and Low suggest that so-called *Asian values* are actually nothing more than Chinese values, and that these in any case parallel Weber's Protestant work ethic (1998, p. 534). (In the context of western Weberian sociology, it is well known that Protestant ethics based on frugality and asceticism have been influential in the entrepreneurial success of modern capitalism.)

Dr Mahathir, too, has invoked the qualities of Asians, and particularly Malaysians, in bringing about the *Asian economic miracle*. However, he has been quick to blame western interference for conspiring against Asia during the 1997-98 financial crisis. In the light of diminishing sovereignty of national governments from globalisation and technological change, Dr Mahathir warns of the dangers and challenges posed by globalisation, and the need for developing countries to acquire the knowledge and skills of the Information Age in order to enable them to catch up with the developed countries (Bernama, 27 June 2000). But despite Dr Mahathir's criticism of globalisation[6], Malaysia - which has one of the highest ratios of exports to GDP (mostly in electronics) - has clearly benefited from it, as the majority of its exports are to the United States, Japan, Europe and Singapore.

It is obvious that globalisation is seen by the South-East Asian political elite as an excuse to find common grounds for countries with diverse ethnic, cultural and political environments, and to provide some justification for authoritarianism. However, it is the demand-pull conditions of globalisation that have enabled regional trans-border groupings such as the Singapore-Johor agglomeration to embark on the road towards a knowledge-based economy. It remains to be seen, though, whether within the auspices of ASEAN both Singapore and Malaysia will continue to combine an open market environment with social and political cohesion to produce technology-intensive goods for the global market.

6.1.2 Implications for Policy

The main objective in this section is to present some policy implications from the empirical studies in Europe and South-East Asia. Our view of the learning behaviour of knowledge-intensive SMEs in regional agglomerations, derived from the surveys, could affect the way we think about improving and supporting innovative performance and disseminating best practices in a globalised world.

Of course, technological advancement in Europe and South-East Asia depends to a large extent on their specific institutional and historical context. The first important aspect to stress, therefore, is that no unique patterns of technological development or processes of integration exist. The EU, for instance, has adopted a highly developed institutional approach, with supranational powers of co-operation and a rather legalistic attitude. ASEAN, on the other hand, functions as a loose intergovernmental grouping which emphasises relationship building between its member countries, rather than between institutions, as is the case in Europe. As Yeung et al. state, 'ASEAN has had success as a political body, while the EU is known primarily as an economic organisation, although that is beginning to change' (1999, p. 78). The European Commission has developed a rather extensive network of institutions that support knowledge-intensive agglomerations. In ASEAN, the Committee on Science and Technology has only very recently begun to play a role in supporting the grouping's knowledge systems (Konstadakopulos, 2002). Nevertheless, in both regional groupings we see evidence of an emerging knowledge-based economy.

It is difficult to draw conclusions about the effectiveness of institutions, and as a result make policy recommendations, from the empirical investigations in the West of England and Singapore-Johor areas. However, in our search for a new direction for innovation and technology policies, we asked firms' managers in both agglomerations to tell us what should be done to improve the prospects for business innovation in their area. A number of managers in the West of England expressed a desire for less interference from national government and the EU. They complained that 'red tape' - i.e. compliance with national and EU legislation - is a serious hindrance, especially for smaller SMEs. In addition, a number of managers wanted an improved road network, and measures to be taken to alleviate skill shortages, especially in engineering. Paradoxically, the non-participation of Britain in the EMU was not seen as an important issue, except by a very few companies.

A number of company managers in Singapore expressed a desire to see an improvement in the creativity capability of the area. Creativity, a special form of knowledge, is notoriously difficult to quantify, although it can be extremely important for urban agglomerations (Lever, 2000, pp.149-50). Some managers pointed out that improving and upgrading the training of the workforce, by providing more subsidised applied research and attracting more expertise from overseas, could achieve this. The alleviation of skill shortages - especially in electronics engineering - was also considered to be an important priority. Furthermore, some managers expressed a wish for less government regulation and more freedom for improving creativity. As Thurow claims:

> Creativity does not occur when it has to challenge authority. Creativity occurs when there is no authority to challenge - when there is an empty space without order where creativity can grow unmolested.
>
> (1999, p. 104)

It was acknowledged by managers that Singapore's environment is too controlled and regulated (Warschauer, 2001, p. 306), lacking the political liberalism and creative chaos of Britain, and that it should loosen up to allow creative breakthroughs and individual ingenuity to develop. For instance, censorship regulations are stricter than in neighbouring Johor. Singapore, therefore, needs an environment that provides more freedom for its citizens to develop their own morality and choose their own values and lifestyles (Low, 2001, p. 432). In this way it could help to develop the indigenous talent needed for innovation, as well as to continue to attract foreign talent (Konstadakopulos, 2000c, p. 58; Warschauer, 2001, p. 307). Apart from advances in electronics, Singapore has developed a limited culture of innovation and technological capabilities, and is still a centre for trading and brokerage activities (Konstadakopulos, 2002, p. 106).

A number of company managers in Johor wanted to see a more flexible education system that could produce the knowledge workers needed for the design and manufacturing of more sophisticated products. 'Brain drain' is also a problem for Johor, given the fact that a large number of its Technological University graduates prefer a well-paid job in cosmopolitan Singapore than a low-paid one in insular Johor. An additional concern was the need to improve the second-class infrastructure, especially the road and telecommunications network, in order to reduce traffic congestion and provide speedy and reliable access to the Internet.

At the firm level, the aim is to enhance the capability of indigenous firms for co-operation in innovation and for interaction with other economic actors within and outside their milieux. As the cluster analysis has shown, firms differ in their capacity to interact with other companies and support agencies. There are some firms which rely on collective efficiency or collaborative relations with their customers and/or suppliers, and others that are isolates.

We have seen that European collaborators and markets are very important for South-East Asian firms. This emphasises the importance of the European Union in the development of the ASEAN region, and raises the question: what is the role of European firms in the ASEAN countries? Most importantly, European firms are ideal partners for fulfilling ASEAN's need for high technology, skills and innovation. European SMEs are suitable for this role, as they are more inclined to transfer technology and know-how, as well as being more flexible than the European TNCs in adapting to the needs of the ASEAN economy (Sieh, 1999).

This view is reinforced by the replies given by company managers in the Singapore-Johor agglomeration during the course of this study. Their perception of European firms in relation to innovative capability, originality and creativity was very positive. German, Dutch and Swiss firms, in particular, were praised by local managers for their willingness to transfer technology to their Asian partners. The European Union's business environment is also recognised as an excellent source for education, training and manpower development; a number of managers interviewed had graduated from a European university, and so were familiar with it. But it is also acknowledged that the number of partnerships between European and Asian firms is relatively low (Lasserre and Schütte, 1999, p. 219). This contrasts with the dominant presence of Japanese firms, which are notoriously reluctant to transfer technology and promote local staff to top positions. However, their readiness to engage in partnerships provides them with local contacts and direct access to governments in the region. The strong position of Japanese and American firms suggests a need for European ones (particularly SMEs) to augment their presence.

ASEAN companies have now developed confidence, and are deliberately seeking strategic alliances in order to increase their knowledge and learn about new products and manufacturing processes. However, technological learning is a costly, time-consuming and difficult process (Athreye, 1999, p. 745). But this has not prevented Malaysia, for instance, from collaborating with Mitsubishi in developing its national car, the Proton, and establishing a cluster of automobile components industries. There are also opportunities for European firms to learn, especially from companies such as the Port of Singapore Authority and Singapore Airlines, which are pioneers in the introduction of new, sophisticated products and services. From the European Union's policy-makers' perspective, Singapore's educational and infrastructure experience could perhaps be instructive.

Finally, the managers of the sampled firms were asked to say what should be done to develop and improve co-operation in innovation with their European counterparts. The majority felt that they needed to know more about the European Union and European companies, and expressed the desirability of taking part in jointly organised trade shows and exhibitions. Some managers stated that they have already been working successfully with European partners, while others highlighted the need for co-investments, joint ventures and licensing arrangements, acknowledging the high level of technological expertise of European companies. There was also a call for subsidised visits to Europe, and more opportunities for socialisation with European SMEs in order to discuss technological breakthroughs necessary for specialisation in niche markets. The EU and monetary union is largely seen in a positive light, although a few managers of Malaysian companies expressed their displeasure with the EU's import quotas and local content requirements[7].

6.2 Recommendations: Facilitating the Development of Knowledge-intensive Enterprises

In an era of globalisation and regionalisation of economic activity, the policy agendas of both the EU and ASEAN, their member states and constituent regions are being driven by the motive of competitiveness. They are shaped by the economic, social and institutional changes of the international capitalist system, a system that, as we have seen, is subject to transformation to an innovation-driven and knowledge-based economy. Overall, the innovative milieu model is a helpful instrument for identifying how knowledge-intensive SMEs in the West of England and Singapore-Johor interact and learn from each other. We have been able to identify some elements of the type of relations, and local and global linkages and networks that exist among companies, and between companies and regional support institutions. Empirical analysis confirmed the existence of collective efficiency and the value of interdependence of high-technology SMEs, from which enterprises can derive efficiency gains (Archibugi and Simonetti, 1998; Cooke, 2002). Given the importance of knowledge-intensive companies, the degree of collective efficiency (derived from external economies and co-operation) in agglomerations may become an important consideration in the design and implementation of policy measures.

The findings from the West of England support the argument that the regional agglomeration remains the main site for R&D, for both indigenous and foreign firms. In this agglomeration, foreign-owned firms appear to be embedded in the local and regional economy. This is not the case in the Singapore-Johor area, where only indigenous firms have R&D facilities, while foreign-owned companies appear to derive their innovative ideas from the parent or affiliate companies overseas. Moreover, when it comes to the use of regional resources in the form of employing the skilled workforce of the area, indigenous firms make more extensive use of such resources than do their foreign counterparts. These findings would seem to have implications for the development of appropriate policies necessary for the embedding of foreign-owned companies into the host economies of South-East Asia.

A significant outcome of the empirical investigation is the confirmation that the actual functioning of the milieu is based to a large extent on the entrepreneurial action of its various economic and social actors. From our interviews it was possible to establish that human skilled capital is the most important determinant of innovation in regional agglomerations[8]. In particular, some individuals displaying a high degree of entrepreneurial behaviour[9], intellectual curiosity and collaborative propensity had generated breakthrough innovations. Such individuals exhibit many of the attributes of the classical entrepreneurial type: intellectual ability, excellence in their particular scientific or managerial domain, team-building skills, participation in extensive networks, strategic vision and tenacity. However, they are different from classical entrepreneurs in the sense that they do not need to possess exceptional leadership skills or other unique abilities (Christopoulos et al., 1999). This implies that the 'innovation entrepreneurs' are dependent on their regional environment. As entrepreneurship is rooted in the institutional setting of the regional innovation system, it must be treated in a systematic way and be a salient policy aspect in the knowledge-based economy (Ebner, 2000, p. 81).

The two empirical case studies described have also shown that decision-makers in both agglomerations are employing very similar policies to deal with the emerging knowledge-based economy. Their main aim is twofold: first, they intend to accelerate the diffusion of intangibles such as information and knowledge; second, they plan to increase their investment in human and social capital through the adoption of a variety of manpower development initiatives. The current study provides a number of reasons why decision-makers should promote the development of human capital, its creativity and entrepreneurial abilities in order to benefit from globalisation. In addition, there is an urgent need for SMEs in particular to be better supported, in order to increase their global presence and gain access to worldwide technologies, networks, knowledge and skills. The case studies also emphasise the significance of TNCs and skilled immigrants in transferring technology and know-how between different market cultures.

It is important to stress that these are findings from a relatively small sample of firms, in just two regional high-technology agglomerations at different stages of development. If the findings are representative of other agglomerations, however, then they suggest that policies orientated towards facilitating the learning behaviour and innovation-enhancing practices of all SMEs are of great importance. Given the fact that most SMEs are still innovation-averse, a great deal of work remains to be done, in both empirical and theoretical terms. Nevertheless, it is hoped that this book provides a useful European and South-East Asian perspective on the learning behaviour of high-technology SMEs in the global knowledge economy, and will encourage the EU and ASEAN to further develop their co-operation in science and technology in the coming years.

Notes

[1] UMNO has become the most powerful party in the ruling National Front (*Barisan Nasional*) coalition. This coalition is, however, multiracial and consists of 14 parties, such as the MCA, representing the Chinese population, the Indian MIC, and others for smaller minority groups. All of these parties play an important role in the economic management of the country and participate in the policy-making process. Nevertheless, UMNO, headed by the Prime Minister, Dr Mahathir Mohamad, is still clearly the dominant force in Malaysian political and economic life.

[2] Ethnicity is understood as being based on genetic and cultural characteristics.

[3] Rodan, in his comparative analysis of Singapore and Malaysia (2002), argues that the importance of

transparency for markets is relative rather than absolute. It is the political stability and the positive perception of government and bureaucracy, he adds, that explains the high degree of confidence of international investors to Singapore. However, this is not the case in Malaysia, where lack of transparency is of concern.

[4] For a useful discussion on the *Singapore Model*, see, among others, Goh (1999), Low (2001) and Yeoh et al. (2001).

[5] For a critical evaluation of Confucian values in East Asia, see Yao (2001).

[6] For a review and critique of the Eurocentric perspective of globalisation theories, see Vertigans and Sutton (2002). For a discussion on the 'new social risks' derived from the structural change in the labour market of Singapore due to globalisation, see Hsieh and Tseng, (2002).

[7] See section above on ASEAN-EU relations.

[8] A more recent survey of 26 managers in knowledge-intensive companies in the West of England indicates that company executives devote resources to the development and diffusion of knowledge within their organisation and employ a variety of knowledge indicators. These indicators are useful for anticipating and measuring the needs of customers, reviewing the performance of their employees, creating national and international networks and joint ventures, and undertaking pre-competitive research (Konstadakopulos et al., 2001).

[9] Interest in the field of entrepreneurship and small business research has significantly increased in the past decade, both in Europe and in Asia. For a review of the research output of small businesses and entrepreneurship in Europe, see Hisrich and Drnovsek (2002).

Bibliography

Abdullah, F., 'IMS-GT: Johor's Experience' in *Growth Triangles in Southeast Asia: Strategy for Development*, Lim, I., (ed.), (Kuala Lumpur, ISIS, 1996), pp. 191-204.

Amin, A. and Thrift, N., 'Institutional Issues for the European Regions: from Markets and Plans to Socioeconomics and Powers of Association', *Economy and Society*, 24:1 (1995), pp. 41-66.

Antonelli, C., 'Collective Knowledge Communication and Innovation: The Evidence of Technological Districts', *Regional Studies*, 34:6 (2000), pp. 535-547.

APEC, *Survey on Small and Medium Enterprises*, Singapore, APEC Secretariat, 1994.

Archibugi, D. and Simonetti, R., 'Objects and Subjects in Technological Interdependence. Towards a Framework to Monitor Innovation', *International Journal of the Economics of Business*, 5:3 (1998), pp. 295-309.

Ashcroft, B., Dunlop, S. and Love, J. H., 'UK Innovation Policy: A Critique', *Regional Studies*, 29:3 (1995), pp. 307-331.

Asheim, B., 'Towards a Learning Based Strategy for Regional Development: Structural Limits or New Possibilities' paper at 'Regional Frontiers' Conference, Frankfurt (Oder), September 20-23, 1997.

Asian Development Bank, *'Publication Highlights - Asian Development Outlook 1999'*, Manila, Oxford University Press, 1999.

Athreye, S., 'Relative Underdevelopment as a Barrier to Technological Efficiency: A Comparative Study of Ministeel Plants in India and the UK', *Modern Asian Studies*, 33:3 (1999), pp. 733-758.

Athukorala, P-C., 'Swimming against the Tide: Crisis Management in Malaysia' in *Southeast Asia's Economic Crisis*, Arndt, H.W. and Hill, H., (eds.), (Singapore, Institute of Southeast Asian Studies, 1999), pp. 28-40.

Aydalot, P., 'Technological Trajectories and Regional Innovation in Europe' in *High Technology Industry and Innovative Environments: The European Experience*, Aydalot, P. and Keeble, D., (eds.), (London, Routledge, 1988), pp. 22-47.

Aydalot, P., *Milieux Innovateurs en Europe*, Paris, GREMI, 1986.

Aydalot, P. and Keeble, D., (eds.), *High Technology Industry and Innovative Environments: The European Experience*, London, Routledge, 1988.

Beaudry, C., 'Entry, Growth and Patenting in Industrial Clusters: A Study of the Aerospace Industry in the UK', *International Journal of the Economics of Business*, 8:3 (2001), pp. 404-436.

Beck, U., *What is Globalization?*, Cambridge, Polity Press, 2000.

Bellandi, M., 'Italian Industrial Districts: An Industrial Economics Interpretation', *European Planning Studies*, 10:4 (2002), pp. 425-437.

Bergman, E. M., Maier, G. and Tödtling, F., (eds.), *Regions Reconsidered - Economic Networks, Innovation, and Local Development in Industrialised Countries*, London, Mansell Publishing, 1991.

Braczyk, H-J., Cooke, P. and Heidenreich, M., (eds.), *Regional Innovation Systems: The Role of Governance in a Globalized Economy*, London, UCL Press, 1998.

Braddon, D. and Konstadakopulos, D., *'The Challenge of the Single Currency: the Problems Facing Businesses in the South West'*, A Euro Seminar Report, Bristol, Royal Society of Arts, (1999).

Bramanti, A. and Ratti, R., 'The Multi-Faced Dimensions of Local Development' in *The Dynamics of Innovative Regions*, Bramanti, A. and Ratti, R., (eds.), (Aldershot, Ashgate Publishing, 1997), pp. 3-44.

Breslin, S. and Higgott, R., 'Studying Regions: Learning from the Old, Constructing the New', *New Political Economy*, 5:3 (2000), pp. 333-352.

Butchard, R. L., 'A New UK Definition of the High Technology Industries', in *Economic Trends*, February (1987), pp. 82-88.

Calabrese, G., 'Small-Medium Car Suppliers and Behavioural Models in Innovation', in *Technology Analysis & Strategic Management*, 14:2 (2002), pp. 217-225.

Calori, R., 'The Diversity of Management Systems' in *European Management Model: Beyond Diversity*, Calori, R. and De Woot, P., (eds.), (London, Prentice Hall, 1994), pp. 11-30.

Calori, R., Valla, J-P. and De Woot, P., 'Common Characteristics: the Ingredients of European Management', in *European Management Model: Beyond Diversity*, Calori, R. and De Woot, P., (eds.), (London, Prentice Hall, 1994), pp. 31-78.

– Bibliography –

Camagni, R. and Rabellotti. R., 'Footwear Production Systems in Italy: A Dynamic Comparative Analysis' in *The Dynamics of Innovative Regions*, Bramanti, A. and Ratti, R., (eds.), (Aldershot, Ashgate Publishing, 1997), pp. 139-163.

Camagni, R., 'The Concept of Innovative Milieu and its Relevance for Public Policies in European Lagging Regions', *Regional Science*, 74:4 (1995), pp. 317-340.

Camagni, R., 'Introduction: from the Local 'Milieu' to Innovation Through Co-operation Networks' in *Innovation Networks: Spatial Perspectives*, Camagni, R., (ed.), (London, Belhaven Press, 1991), pp. 1-9.

Capello, R., 'Spatial Transfer of Knowledge in High Technology Milieux: Learning Versus Collective Learning Process', *Regional Studies*, 33:4 (1999), pp. 353-365.

Caraça, J., 'The Experience of Technology Policies in Portugal', paper at the Technology Policy and Less Developed Research and Development Systems in Europe Conference, Seville 17-18 October 1997.

Caracostas, P. and Muldur, U., 'Society, the Endless Frontier: Ten Key Ideas', in *The Knowledge-Based Economy - The European Challenges of the 21st Century*, Kuklinski, A., (ed.), (Warsaw, State Committee for Scientific Research, 2000), pp. 13-33.

Castells, M., *The Information Age: Economy, Society and Culture*, 3 Vols, Cambridge, Mass., Blackwell Publishers, 1996.

Chia, S. Y., 'The Asian Financial Crisis: Singapore's Experience and Response' in *Southeast Asia's Economic Crisis*, Arndt, H.W. and Hill, H., (eds.), (Singapore, Institute of Southeast Asian Studies, 1999), pp. 51-66.

Chia, S. Y., 'Singapore: Advanced Production Base and Smart Hub of the Electronics Industry' in *Multinationals and East Asian Integration*, Dobson, W. And Chia, S. Y. (eds.), (Ottawa, International Research Centre, 1997), pp. 31-61.

Chia, S. Y., 'Sijori GT: Challenges and Opportunities' in *Growth Triangles in Southeast Asia: Strategy for Development*, Lim, I., (ed.), (Kuala Lumpur, ISIS, 1996), pp. 173-190.

Chin, C. B. N., 'The State of the 'State' in Globalisation: Social Order and Economic Restructuring in Malaysia', *Third World Quarterly*, 21:6 (2000), pp. 1035-1057.

Christopoulos, D. and Konstadakopulos, D., 'Innovative Milieux and Regional Networks: The Governance of Technological Change and Learning in Five European Regions' in *The Changing Map of Europe - The Trajectory Berlin-Pozna_-Warsaw*, Doma_ski, R., (ed.), (Warsaw, Friedrich Ebert Stiftung, 1999), pp. 251-268.

Christopoulos, D., Shaw, I. and Konstadakopulos, D., 'Innovation Entrepreneurs and Innovation Networks: Case Study of a Highly Innovative Firm' in *Proceedings of the 22nd ISBA National Small Firms & Policy Research Conference*, Volume 1, pp. 291-314, Leeds, Leeds Metropolitan University, 1999.

Clad, J., *Behind the Myth: Business Money and Power in South East Asia*, London: Unwin Hyman Ltd, 1989.

Cooke, P., 'Biotechnology Clusters as Regional, Sectoral Innovation Systems', *International Regional Science Review*, 25:1 (2002), pp 8-37.

Cooke, P., Boekholt, P. and Tödtling, F., *The Governance of Innovation in Europe: Regional Perspectives on Global Competitiveness*, London, Pinter, 2000.

Da Cunha, D., 'A Multiplicity of Approaches to Foreign and Defence Policy' in *Singapore - The Year in Review 1997*, Mahizhnan, A. (ed.), (Singapore, Times Academic Press, (1998), pp. 60-75.

Dalum, D., Johnson, B. and Lundvall, B.A., 'Public Policy in the Learning Society' in *National Systems of Innovation: Towards a Theory of Innovation and Interactive Learning*, Lundvall, B. A., (ed.), (Pinter, London, 1992), pp. 298-317.

De Bernardy, M., 'Reactive and Proactive Local Territory: Co-operation and Community in Grenoble', *Regional Studies*, 33:4 (1999), pp. 343-352.

De Propis, L., 'Systematic Flexibility, Production Fragmentation and Cluster Governance', *European Planning Studies*, 9:6 (2001), pp. 739-753.

Debrah, Y. A., McGovern, I. and Budhwar, P., 'Complementarity or Competition: the Development of Human Resources in a South-East Asian Growth Triangle: Indonesia, Malaysia and Singapore', *International Journal of Human Resource Management*, 11:2 (2000), pp. 314-335.

Department of Trade and Industry (DTI), *Our Competitive Future: Building the Knowledge Driven Economy*, London, HMSO, 1998.

Diez, M. A., 'The Evaluation of Regional Innovation and Cluster Policies: Towards a Participatory Approach', *European Planning Studies*, 9:7 (2001), pp. 902-923.

Dosi, G., Freeman, C., Nelson, R., Silverberg, G. and Soete, L., *Technical Change and Economic Theory*, London, Pinter, 1987.

Drèze, J., 'Regions of Europe: a Feasible Status, to be Discussed' in *Economic Policy*, 17:2 (1993), pp. 266-293.

Dupuy, C. and Gilly, J. P., 'Collective Learning and Territorial Dynamics: a New Approach to the Relations between Industrial Groups and Territories', *Environment and Planning A*, 28:9 (1996), pp. 1603-1616.

Eaton, J., Gutierrez, E. and Kortum, S., 'European Technology Policy', *Economic Policy*, 13:27 (1998), pp 403-438.

Ebner, A., 'Systems of Innovation Between Globalisation and Transformation: Policy Implications for the Support of Schumpeterian Entrepreneurship' in *The Knowledge-Based Economy - The Global Challenges of the 21st Century*, Kuklinski, A. and Orlowski, W., (eds.), (Warsaw, State Committee for Scientific Research, 2000), pp. 80-99.

Economic Development Board, *Growing a Knowledge-Based Economy*, Yearbook 1997/98, Singapore, EDB, 1999.

Economic Planning Unit, *Eighth Malaysian Plan (2001-2005)*, Kuala Lumpur, Prime Minister's Department, 2001.

EIU, *Country Report: Singapore*, Quarterly Report: 1st quarter 1998, London, The Economist Intelligence Unit, 1999.

Enterprise and Prism Research, *'Review of Business Support in the South West Region'*, Final Report, March 2000.

Eser, T. and Konstadakopulos, D., 'Power Shifts in the European Union? The Case of Spatial Planning', *European Planning Studies*, 8:6 (2000), pp. 783-798.

Feser, E. J., 'Old and New Theories of Industry Clusters', in *Clusters and Regional Specialisation*, Steiner, M., (ed.) (London, Pion Ltd, 1998), pp. 18-40.

Forster, A., 'The European Union in South-East Asia: Continuity and Change in Turbulent Times', *International Affairs*, 75:4 (1999), pp. 743-758.

Freeman, C., 'The "National System of Innovation" in Historical Perspective', *Cambridge Journal of Economics*, 19:1 (1995), pp. 5-24.

Freeman, N., 'ASEAN Investment Area: Progress and Challenges' in *ASEAN Beyond the Regional Crisis: Challenges and Initiatives*, Than, M., (ed.), (Singapore, Institute of Southeast Asian Studies, 2001), pp. 80-125.

Freeman, N. and Hew, D., 'Introductory Overview: Rethinking the East Asian Development *Model'*, *ASEAN Economic Bulletin*, 19:1 (2002), pp. 1-5.

Friedman, J., 'The Industrial Transition: A Comprehensive Approach to Regional Development' in *Regions Reconsidered - Economic Networks, Innovation, and Local Development in Industrialised Countries*, Bergman, E. M., Maier, G. and Tödtling, F., (eds.), (London, Mansell Publishing, 1991), pp. 160-177.

Galar, R., 'Knowledge Economy as an Antagonist' in *The Knowledge-Based Economy - The European Challenges of the 21st Century*, Kuklinski, A., (ed.), (Warsaw, State Committee for Scientific Research, 2000), pp. 288-291.

Garofoli, G., 'New Firm Formation and Regional Development: The Italian Case', *Regional Studies*, 28:4 (1994), pp. 381-393.

Gertler, M., Wolfe, D. and Garkut, D., 'No place like home? The embeddedness of innovation in a regional economy', *Review of International Political Economy*, 7:4 (2000), pp. 688-718.

Giddens, A., *BBC Reith Lecture on Globalisation*, London, BBC, 1999. http://news6.thdo.bbc.co.uk/hi/english/static/events/reith_99/week1/week1.htm, accessed 23 August 2000.

Goh, C. B., 'Climbing up the Technological Ladder: Some Issues and Problems in ASEAN' in *Development and Challenge: Southeast Asia in the New Millennium*, Wong, T-C. and Singh M., (eds.), (Singapore, Times Media Private Ltd, 1999), pp. 99-126.

Gordon, R., 'Innovation, Industrial Networks and High-Technology Regions' in *Innovation Networks: Spatial Perspectives*, Camagni, R., (ed.), (London, Belhaven, 1991), pp. 174-195.

Grabher, G., 'Rediscovering the Social in the Economics of Interfirm Relations' in *The Embedded Firm: On Socio-economics of Industrial Networks*, Grabher, G., (ed.), (London, Routledge, 1993), pp. 1-31.

Grabher, G. and Stark, D., 'Organising Diversity: Evolutionary Theory, Network Analysis and Postsocialism', *Regional Studies*, 31:5 (1997), pp. 533-554.

Granovetter, M., 'Economic Action and Social Structure: The Problem of Embeddedness', *American Journal of Sociology*, 31:5 (1985), pp. 481-510.

Gregersen, B. and Johnson, B., 'Learning Economies, Innovation Systems and European Integration', *Regional Studies*, 31:5 (1997), pp. 479-490.

Grunsven, L. van, Heijden, M. van der and Sluys, P., 'Foreign Investment and Industrial Structure in Johor, Malaysia', *Report Series 1995*, Utrecht, Utrecht University, 1995a.

Grunsven, L. van, Egeraat, C. van and Meijsen, S., 'New Manufacturing Establishments and Regional Economy in Johor - Production Linkages, Employment and Labour Fields', *Report Series 1995*, Utrecht, Utrecht University, 1995b.

Hadjimanolis, A., 'An Investigation of Innovation Antecedents in Small Firms in the Context of a Small Developing Country', *R&D Management*, 30:3 (2000), pp. 235-245.

Haley, U. and Low, L., 'Crafted Culture: Governmental Sculpting of Modern Singapore and Effects on Business Environments', *Journal of Organisational Change and Management*, 11:6 (1998), pp. 530-553.

Hall, B. H., 'The Assessment: Technology Policy', *Oxford Review of Economic Policy*, 19:1 (2002), pp. 1-9.

Hall, P., *The University and the City*, Dordrecht, Kluwer Academic Publishers, 1997.

Hamilton, G., 'Culture and Organization in Taiwan's Market Economy' in *Market Cultures: Society and Morality in the New Asian Capitalisms*, Hefner, R., (ed.), (Colorado, Westview Press, 1998), pp. 41-77.

Hamilton-Hart, N., 'The Singapore State Revisited', *The Pacific Review*, 13:2 (2000), pp. 195-216.

Harris, L., Coles, A-M. and Dickson, K., 'Building Innovation Networks: Issues of Strategy and Expertise', *Technology Analysis & Strategic Management*, 12:2 (2000), pp. 229-241.

Hay, C. and Watson, M., 'Globalisation: 'Sceptical' Notes on the 1999 Reith Lectures', *Political Quarterly*, 70:4 (1999), pp. 418-425.

Hefner, R., 'Introduction' in *Market Cultures: Society and Morality in the New Asian Capitalisms*, Hefner, R., (ed.), (Colorado, Westview Press, 1998), pp. 1-38.

Heijs, J., 'The Transferability of the German Model of Technology Policy and Less Developed R&D Systems in Europe', paper presented at the Technology Policy and Less Developed Research and Development Systems in Europe Conference, Seville 17-18 October 1997.

Helmsing, A. H. J., 'Externalities, Learning and Governance: New Perspectives on Local Economic Development', *Development and Change*, 32:2 (2001), pp. 277-308.

Hendry, C., Brown, J. and Defillippi, R., 'Regional Clustering of High Technology-based Firms: Opto-electronics in Three Countries', *Regional Studies*, 34:2 (2000), pp. 129-144.

Higgott, R., 'The Political Economy of Globalisation in East Asia' in *Globalisation and the Asia-Pacific: Contested Territories*, Olds, K., Dicken, P., Kelly P. F., Kong, L. and Yeung H. W-C., (eds.), (London, Routledge, 1999), pp. 91-106.

Hine, R., 'Bridging Two Continents: EU-ASEAN Trade and Investment' in *The European Union and ASEAN: Trade and Investment Issues*, Strange, R., Slater, J. and Molteni, C., (eds.), (Basingstoke, Macmillan Press 2000), pp. 9-32.

Hisrich, R. D. and Drnovsek, M., 'Entrepreneurship and Small Business Research - a European Perspective', *Journal of Small Business and Enterprise Development*, 9:2 (2002), pp. 172-222.

Hobday, M., *Innovation in East Asia*, Cheltenham, Edward Elgar, 1997.

Hobson, J. M. and Ramesh, M., 'Globalisation Makes of States What States Make of It: Between Agency and Structure in the State/Globalisation Debate', *New Political Economy*, 7:1 (2002), pp. 5-22.

Hofstede, G. H., *Culture's Consequences: International Differences in Work-related Values*, Beverly Hills, Sage Publications, 1980.

Howells, J., 'Tacit Knowledge, Innovation and Economic Geography', *Urban Studies*, 39:5-6 (2002), pp. 871-884.

Hsieh, Y-L. and Tseng, S-F., 'The Welfare State in the Information Age: Hollowing out or Restructuring in the Changing Labour Market in Singapore?', *International Journal of Human Resource Management*, 13:3 (2002), pp. 501-521.

Hudson, R., 'The Learning Economy, The Learning Firm and the Learning Region', *European Urban and Regional Studies*, 6:1 (1999), pp. 59-72.

Jessop, B. and Sum, N-L., 'An Entrepreneurial City in Action: Hong Kong's Emerging Strategies in and for (Inter)Urban Competition', *Urban Studies*, 37:12 (2000), pp. 2287-2313.

Johanson, U., Mårtensson, M. and Skoog, M., 'Measuring to Understand Intangible Performance Drivers', *The European Accounting Review*, 10:3 (2001), pp. 407-437.

Jones, A. and Lall, A., 'A Comparative Record of Technological Capability in ASEAN Countries' in *Technovation*, 18:4 (1998), pp. 263-274.

Kamann, D-J., 'Policies for Dynamic Innovative Networks in Innovative Milieux' in *The Dynamics of Innovative Regions*, Bramanti, A. and Ratti, R., (eds.), (Aldershot, Ashgate Publishing, 1997), pp. 367-391.

– Bibliography –

Kamann, D-J., 'The Distribution of Dominance in Networks and its Spatial Implications', in *Regions Reconsidered - Economic Networks, Innovation, and Local Development in Industrialized Countries*, Bergman, E. M., Maier, G. and Tödtling, F., (eds.), (London, Mansell, 1991), pp. 30-45.

Kanter, R. M., *World Class: Thriving Locally in the Global Economy*, London, Simon and Schuster, 1995.

Keeble, D., Lawson, C., Lawton-Smith, H., Moore, B. and Wilkinson, F., 'Collective Learning Processes and Inter-Firm Networking in Innovative High-Technology Regions' paper at 'Regional Frontiers' Conference, Frankfurt (Oder), September 20-23 1997.

Keeble, D., Lawson, C., Moore, B. and Wilkinson, F., 'Collective Learning Processes, Networking and "Institutional Thickness" in the Cambridge Region', *Regional Studies*, 33:4 (1999), pp. 319-332.

Khalafalla, Y. K. and Webb, J. A., 'Export-led Growth and Structural Change: Evidence from Malaysia', *Applied Economics*, 33:13 (2001), pp. 1703-1715.

Kirat, T. and Lung, Y., 'Innovation and Proximity: Territories as Loci of Collective Learning Processes', *European Urban and Regional Studies*, 6:1 (1999), pp. 27-38.

Klomp, L. and van Leeuwen, G., 'Linking Innovation and Firm Performance: A New Approach', *International Journal of the Economics of Business*, 8:3 (2001), pp. 343-364.

Knoke, D., *Political Networks: The Structural Perspective*, Cambridge, Cambridge University Press, 1990.

Koh, T., 'Size is not Destiny' in *Singapore: Re-engineering Success*, Mahizhnan, A. and Yuan L. T., (eds.), (Singapore, The Institute of Policy Studies and Oxford University Press, 1998), pp. 172-180.

Konstadakopulos, D., 'The Challenge of Technological Development for ASEAN: Intraregional and International Co-operation', *ASEAN Economic Bulletin*, 19:1 (2002), pp. 101-111.

Konstadakopulos, D., 'The Regions and Their Firms in the Perspective of Global Change' in *Globalisation: Experiences and Prospects*, Bünz, H. and Kuklinski, A., (eds.), (Warsaw, Friedrich Ebert Stiftung, 2001), pp. 306-324.

Konstadakopulos, D., 'The Evolution, Structure and Process of Technological Innovation Policy in Peripheral European Regions: Evidence from the South West of

England, Catalonia and Western Greece', *Regional and Federal Studies*, 10:3 (2000a), pp. 61-86.

Konstadakopulos, D., 'Milieux innovateurs et apprentissage dans le Sud-Ouest de l'Angleterre' in *Innovations, Cahiers d'Economie de l'Innovation*, 11:1 (2000b), pp. 139-154.

Konstadakopulos, D., 'Learning Behaviour and Co-operation of Small High Technology Firms in the ASEAN Region: Some Evidence from the Singapore-Johor Agglomeration', *ASEAN Economic Bulletin*, 17:1 (2000c), pp. 48-59.

Konstadakopulos, D., 'A Report on Learning for Innovation in the South West of England and South Wales: Supporting and Helping Small- and Medium-sized Enterprises to Improve Performance and Competitiveness', Bristol, University of the West of England, 1997.

Konstadakopulos, D., Revilla Diez, J., Kockel, U. and Mildahn, B., 'Knowledge Companies in Britain and Germany: A Common Response to the Challenges of the Emerging Knowledge-based Economy?', a report to the Anglo-German Foundation for the Study of Industrial Society, London, 2001, (on-line www.agf.org.uk/pubs/publications.rtm).

Konstadakopulos, D., Christopoulos D. and Cannon, J., 'Regional Strategies for the Future: Growing a Knowledge-Based Economy in the West of England and Singapore-Johor Agglomerations' in *The Knowledge-Based Economy - The Global Challenges of the 21st Century*, Kuklinski, A. and Orlowski, W., (eds.), (Warsaw, State Committee for Scientific Research, 2000), pp. 274-287.

Konstadakopulos, D., Artal-Tur, A. and Middleditch, A-M., 'The Regionalisation of Innovation Policy in Southern Europe' in *Contemporary Political Studies*, Dobson, A. and Stanyer, J., (eds.), (Nottingham, PSA, Vol. 1, 1998), pp. 56-71.

Konstadakopulos, D. and Christopoulos, D., 'Innovative Milieux and Networks, Technological Change and Learning in European Regions: Technology Policy and Innovation Strategies', paper presented at the Technology Policy and Less Developed Research and Development Systems in Europe Conference, Seville 17-18 October 1997.

Kuklinski, A., (ed.), *The Knowledge-Based Economy - The European Challenges of the 21st Century*, Warsaw, State Committee for Scientific Research, 2000a.

Kuklinski, A., 'The Future of Europe - Four Dilemmas and Five Scenarios: A Challenge for Prospective Thinking' in *The Knowledge-Based Economy - The European Challenges of the 21st Century*, Kuklinski, A., (ed.), (Warsaw, State Committee for Scientific Research, 2000b), pp. 141-148.

– Bibliography –

Kuklinski, A. and Orlowski, W., (eds.), *The Knowledge-Based Economy - The Global Challenges of the 21st Century*, Warsaw, State Committee for Scientific Research, 2000.

Lagendijk, A., 'New Ways for Local and Regional Economic Development' in *Contemporary Political Studies*, Dobson, A. and Stanyer, J., (eds.), (Nottingham, PSA, Vol. 1, 1998), pp. 313-340.

Lasserre P. and Schütte H., *Strategies for Asia Pacific: Beyond the Crisis*, London, Macmillan, 1999.

Lawson, C., 'Territorial Clustering and High-technology Innovation: From Industrial Districts to Innovative Milieux', Working Paper 54, University of Cambridge, 1997.

Lawson, C. and Lorenz, E., 'Collective Learning, Tacit Knowledge and Regional Innovative Capacity', *Regional Studies*, 33:4 (1999), pp. 305-317.

Leadbeater, C., *Living on Thin Air: The New Economy*, London, Penguin 1999.

Leifer, M., 'Singapore in Regional and Global Context: Sustaining Exceptionalism' in *Singapore: Re-engineering Success*, Mahizhnan, A. and Lee Tsao Y., (eds.), (Singapore, Oxford University Press, 1998), pp. 19-30.

Lever, W. F., 'Correlating the Knowledge-base of Cities with Economic Growth', *Urban Studies*, 39:5-6 (2002), pp. 871-884.

Lever, W. F., 'Measuring the Comparative Advantage of the Knowledge Base' in *The Knowledge-Based Economy - The Global Challenges of the 21st Century*, Kuklinski, A. and Orlowski, W., (eds.), (Warsaw, State Committee for Scientific Research, 2000), pp. 139-151.

Li, T., 'The Singapore Malay Problem and Entrepreneurship Reconsidered' in *Market Cultures: Society and Morality in the New Asian Capitalisms*, Hefner, R., (ed.), (Colorado, Westview Press, 1998), pp. 147-172.

Lim, I., (ed.), *Growth Triangles in Southeast Asia: Strategy for Development*, Kuala Lumpur, ISIS, 1996.

Lim, I. and Nesadurai, H., 'Managing the Malaysian Industrial Economy - The Policy and Reform Process for Industrialization' in *Industrial Policies in East Asia*, Masuyama, S., Vandenbrink, D. and Chia, S. Y., (eds.), (Tokyo/Singapore, Nomura Research Institute and Institute of Southeast Asian Studies, 1997), pp. 185-215.

Ljungkvist, T., *'ASEAN and EU: A Study on Trade and Specialisation, Minor Field Study Series'*, No. 89, Lund, University of Lund, 1998.

Locke, R., *Remaking the Italian Economy*, London, Cornell University Press, 1995.

Lorenzen, M., 'Localized Learning and Policy: Academic Advice on Enhancing Regional Competitiveness through Learning', *European Planning Studies*, 9:2 (2001), pp. 163-185.

Low, L., 'The Singapore Developmental State in the New Economy and Polity', *The Pacific Review*, 14:3 (2001), pp. 411-441.

Low, L., 'Overall Reassessment of the IMS-GT Triangle' in *Indonesia, Malaysia, Singapore, Growth Triangle: Borderless Region for Sustainable Progress*, Awang, A., Salim, M. and Haldare, J., (eds.), (Johor, Malaysia: Institute Sultan Iskandar, 1998), pp. 44-55.

Lundvall, B. A., (ed.), *National Systems of Innovation: Towards a Theory of Innovation and Interactive Learning*, London, Pinter, 1992.

Lundvall, B. A. and Johnson, B., 'The Learning Economy', *Journal of Industry Studies*, 1:2 (1994), pp. 23-42.

Mackie, J., 'Business Success among Southeast Asian Chinese' in *Market Cultures: Society and Morality in the New Asian Capitalisms*, Hefner, R., (ed.), (Colorado, Westview Press, 1998), pp. 129-146.

Maillat, D., 'The Innovation Process and the Role of the Milieu' in *Regions Reconsidered - Economic Networks, Innovation, and Local Development in Industrialised Countries*, Bergman, E. M., Maier, G. and Tödtling, F., (eds.), (London, Mansell Publishing, 1991), pp. 103-118.

Malecki, E. J., 'Hard and Soft Networks for Urban Competitiveness', *Urban Studies*, 39:5-6 (2002), pp. 929-945.

Mallet, V., *The Trouble with Tigers: The Rise and Fall of South-East Asia*, London, Harper Collins, 1999.

Martin, R. and Sunley, P., 'Deconstructing Clusters: Chaotic Concept or Policy Panacea?', Proceedings of the Conference on Regionalising the Knowledge Economy, pp. 8-13, London, Regional Studies Association, 2001.

Masuyama, S., 'The Evolving Nature of Industrial Policy in East Asia: Liberalization, Upgrading, and Integration' in *Industrial Policies in East Asia*, Masuyama, S., Vandenbrink, D. and Chia, S. Y., (eds.), (Tokyo/Singapore: Nomura Research Institute and Institute of Southeast Asian Studies, 1997), pp. 3-18.

Matthiessen, C. W., Schwarz, A. W. and Find, S., 'The Top-level Global Research System, 1997-99: Centres, Networks and Nodality. An Analysis Based on Bibliometric Indicators', *Urban Studies*, 39:5-6 (2002), pp. 903-927.

Matthiessen, C. W. and Schwarz, A. W., 'Knowledge Centres of Europe: An Analysis of Research Strength and Patterns of Specialization Based on Bibliometric Indicators' in *The Knowledge-Based Economy - The Global Challenges of the 21st Century*, Kuklinski, A. and Orlowski, W., (eds.), (Warsaw, State Committee for Scientific Research, 2000), pp. 47-67.

Meeus, M. T. H., Oerlemans, L. A. G. and Hage, J., 'Sectoral Patterns of Interactive Learning: An Empirical Exploration of a Case in a Dutch Region' in *Technology Analysis & Strategic Management*, 13:3 (2001), pp. 407-431.

Miozzo, M. and Montobbio, F., 'The Evolution of Knowledge Bases, Patterns of Location and Industrial Dynamics: A Reassessment of the Product and Industry Life Cycle Models' in *The Knowledge-Based Economy - The Global Challenges of the 21st Century*, Kuklinski, A. and Orlowski, W., (eds.), (Warsaw: State Committee for Scientific Research, (2000), pp. 114-138.

Mitra, J., 'Making Connections: Innovation and Collective Learning in Small Businesses', *Education and Training*, 42:4/5 (2000), pp. 228-236.

Mohamed, J., 'Johor: The Southern Gateway for Investment Opportunities in Malaysia' in *Indonesia, Malaysia, Singapore, Growth Triangle: Borderless Region for Sustainable Progress*, Awang, A., Salim, M. and Haldare, J., (eds.), (Johor, Malaysia, Institute Sultan Iskandar, 1998), pp. 153-159.

Morgan, K., 'The Learning Region: Institutions, Innovation and Regional Renewal', *Regional Studies*, 31:5 (1997), pp. 491-503.

Murshed, S. M., 'Patterns of East Asian Trade and Intra-Industry Trade in Manufactures', *Journal of the Asia Pacific Economy*, 6:1 (2001), pp. 99-123.

Nahm, A. Y. and Vonderembse, M. A., 'Theory Development: an Industrial/Post Industrial Perspective on Manufacturing', *International Journal of Production*, 40:9 (2002), pp. 2067-2095.

Natarajan, S. and Tan, J. M., *The Impact of MNC Investments in Malaysia, Singapore and Thailand*, Singapore: Institute of South East Asian Studies, 1992.

National Statistics, *Regional Competitiveness Indicators*, London, Office for National Statistics, Table 9 (b), May 2002, p. 52.

Nelson, R. and Winter, G., *An Evolutionary Theory of Economic Change*, London, Belknap Press of Harvard University Press, 1982.

Ng, I. V. and Wong P. K., 'The Growth Triangle: A Market Driven Response', Tokyo Club Foundation for Global Studies, mimeo, (1991), pp. 123-154.

OECD, *The New Economy: Beyond the Hype*, Paris, Organisation for Economic Co-operation and Development, 2001.

OECD, 'Knowledge Intensive Services - What is their Role?', paper for the OECD Business and Industry Policy Forum on Realising the Potential of the Service Economy: Facilitating Growth, Innovation and Competition, Paris, 28 September 1999.

OECD, *The Knowledge-based Economy*, Paris, Organisation for Economic Co-operation and Development, 1996.

Oerlemans, L. A. G., Meeus, M. T. H. and Boekema, F. W. M., 'On the Spatial Embeddedness of Innovation Networks: An Exploration of the Proximity Effect', *Tijdschrift voor Economische en Sociale Geografie*, 92:1 (2001), pp. 60-75.

Olds, K., Dicken, P., Kelly, P., Kong, L. and Yeung, H. W-C., (eds.), *Globalisation and Asia-Pacific*, London, Routledge, 1999.

Paci, R. and Usai, S., 'Technological Enclaves and Industrial Districts: An Analysis of the Regional Distribution of Innovative Activity in Europe', *Regional Studies*, 34:2 (2000), pp. 97-114.

Palmujoki, E., 'EU-ASEAN Relations: Reconciling Two Different Agendas' in *Contemporary Southeast Asia*, 19:3 (1997), pp. 269-285.

Parker, R., 'The Myth of the Entrepreneurial Economy: Employment and Innovation in Small Firms' in *Work, Employment & Society*, 15: 2 (2001), pp. 373-384.

Peyrache-Gadeau, V., 'Dynamic and Structural Changes of Localised Productive Systems' in *The Dynamics of Innovative Regions*, Bramanti, A. and Ratti, R., (eds.), (Aldershot, Ashgate Publishing, 1997), pp. 295-319.

Picard, J. and Konstadakopulos, D., 'Brittany: Endogenous Development and Socio-political Networks', *Regions*, 20:8 (1997), pp. 31-36.

Pinch, S. and Henry, N., 'Paul Krugman's Geographical Economics, Industrial Clustering and the British Motor Sport Industry', *Regional Studies*, 33:9 (1999), pp. 815-827.

– Bibliography –

Porter, M., 'Competitive Advantage, Agglomeration Economies, and Regional Policy', *International Regional Science Review*, 19:1&2 (1996), pp. 85-94.

Porter, M., *The Competitive Advantage of the Nations*, London, Macmillan, 1990.

Putman, R., (with Nanetti, R. and Leonardi, R.), *Making Democracy Work: Civic Traditions in Modern Italy*, Princeton, Princeton University Press, 1993.

Rabellotti, R., *External Economies and Co-operation in Industrial Districts*, London, Macmillan, 1997.

Raco, M., 'The Social Relations of Organisational Activity and the New Local Governance in the UK', *Urban Studies*, 39:3 (2002), pp. 437-456.

Reynolds, C., 'A Conceptual Model of Global Business Growth in Southeast Asia', *Journal of Asia Pacific Economy*, 6:1 (2001), pp. 76-98.

Rodan, G., 'Do Markets Need Transparency? The Pivotal Cases of Singapore and Malaysia', *New Political Economy*, 7:1 (2002), pp. 23-47.

RSA, 'Regionalising the Knowledge Economy', Proceedings of the Conference of the Regional Studies Association, Seaford: Regional Studies Association, 2001.

Schlossstein, S., *Asia's New Little Dragons: The Dynamic Emergence of Indonesia, Thailand, and Malaysia*, Chicago, Contemporary Books, Inc., 1991.

Seely Brown, J. and Duguid, P., *The Social Life of Information*, Boston, Harvard Business School Press, 2000.

Selover, D., 'International Interdependence and Business Cycle Transmission in ASEAN', *Journal of the Japanese and International Economies*, 13:2 (1999), pp. 230-253.

Sengenberger, W. and Pyke, F., 'Industrial Districts and Local Economic Regeneration: Research and Policy Issues' in *Industrial Districts and Local Economic Regeneration*, Pyke, F. and Sengenberger, W., (eds.), (Geneva, ILO Publications, 1992), pp. 3-29.

Sieh Lee, M. L., 'Emerging Business Opportunities from ASEAN-Europe Integration' in *ASEAN & EU: Forging New Linkages and Strategic Alliances*, Chia, S. Y. and Tan, J. L .H., (eds.), (Singapore, Institute of Southeast Asia Studies, 1999), pp. 150-165.

Sieh Lee, M. L. and Yew Siew, Y., 'Malaysia: Electronics, Autos, and Trade-Investment Nexus' in *Multinationals and East Asian Integration*, Dobson, W. and Chia, S. Y., (eds.), (Ottawa, International Research Centre, 1997), pp. 131-152.

Simandjuntak, D., 'EU-ASEAN Relationship: Trends and Issues' in *ASEAN in the New Asia*, Chia, S.Y. and Pacini, M., (eds.), (Singapore, Institute of Southeast Asian Studies, 1998), pp. 92-117.

Singapore Manufacturers' Association (SMA), *'Survey Report on the Johor-Singapore-Riau Growth Triangle'*, SMA Research Division, September 1992.

Slater, J., 'Conclusions', in *The European Union and ASEAN: Trade and Investment Issues*, Strange, R., Slater, J. and Molteni, C., (eds.), (Basingstoke, Macmillan Press, 2000), pp. 238-240.

Soete, L., 'ICTs, Knowledge Work and Employment: the Challenges of Europe', *International Labour Review*, 140:2 (2001), pp. 143-163.

Steiner, M., 'The Discreet Charm of Clusters: an Introduction' in *Clusters and Regional Specialisation*, Steiner, M., (ed.), (London, Pion Ltd, 1998), pp. 1-17.

Sternberg, R., 'Innovation Networks and Regional Development - Evidence from the European Regional Innovation Survey (ERIS): Theoretical Concepts, Methodological Approach, Empirical Basis and Introduction to the Theme Issue', *European Planning Studies*, 8:4 (2000), pp. 389-407.

Sternberg, R., 'Regional Growth Theories and High-Tech Regions', *International Journal of Urban and Regional Research*, 20:3 (1996a), pp. 518-538.

Sternberg, R., 'Technology Policies and the Growth of Regions: Evidence from Four Countries', *Small Business Economics*, 8:1 (1996b), pp. 75-86.

Storper, M., 'The Resurgence of Regional Economies, Ten Years Later: The Regions as a Nexus of Untraded Interdependencies', *European Urban and Regional Studies*, 2:3 (1995), pp. 191-221.

Storper, M., 'Regional "Worlds" of Production: Learning and Innovation in the Technology Districts of France, Italy and the USA', *Regional Studies*, 27:5 (1993), pp. 433-455.

Streeck, W. and Schmitter, P., 'Community, Market, State and Association? The Perspective Contribution of Interest Governance to Social Order' in *Markets, Hierarchies and Networks*, Thompson, G., Frances, J., Levacic, R. and Mitchell, J., (eds.), (London, Sage, 1991), pp. 227-241.

SWERDA, 'Regional Strategy for the South West of England, 2000-2010' Exeter, South West of England Regional Development Agency, (brochure) 2000.

– Bibliography –

Tan, G., *ASEAN Economic Development and Co-operation*, Singapore, Times Academic Press, 1996.

Tang, M. and Thant, M., 'Growth Triangles: Conceptual and Operational Considerations' in *Growth Triangles in Asia: A New Approach to Regional Economic Cooperation*, Thant, M., Tang, M. and Kakazu, H., (eds.), (Hong Kong: Oxford University Press, 1994), pp. 23-48.

Teubal M., 'A Catalytic and Evolutionary Approach to Horizontal Technology Policies (HTPs)' in *Research Policy*, 25:6 (1997), pp. 1161-1188.

Than, M., 'Overview' in *Indonesia-Malaysia-Thailand Growth Triangle: Theory to Practice*, Than, M. and Tang, M., (eds.), (Manila, Asian Development Bank, 1996), pp. 1-27.

Than, M. and Tang, M., (eds.), *Indonesia-Malaysia-Thailand growth Triangle: Theory to Practice*, Manila, Asian Development Bank, 1996.

Thornton, J. and Goglio, A., 'Regional Bias and Intra-regional Trade in Southeast Asia', *Applied Economics Letters*, 9:4 (2002), pp. 205-208.

Thrift, N., 'It's the Romance, not the Finance, that Makes the Business Worth Pursuing: Disclosing a New Market Culture', *Economy and Society*, 30:4 (2001), pp. 412-432.

Thurow, L. C., *Building Wealth: The New Rules for Individuals, Companies, and Nations in a Knowledge-based Economy*, New York, Harper Collins, 1999.

Thurow, L. C., *The Future of Capitalism: How Today's Economic Forces Shape Tomorrow's World*, New York, William Morrow, 1996.

UNCTAD, *World Development Report 2001: Promoting Linkages*, New York and Geneva, United Nations, 2001.

UWE, *Facilitating the Learning Behaviour of Small Innovative Firms*, Survey Report, Bristol, University of the West of England, 1999.

Vellinga, M., 'Economic Internationalisation and Regional Response: the Case of North Eastern Mexico', *Tijdschrift voor Economische en Sociale Geografie*, 91:3 (2000), pp. 293-307.

Vence, X., Guntín, X. and Rodil, O., 'Determinants of the Uneven Regional Participation of Firms in European Technology Programmes. The "Low R&D Trap" ', *European Planning Studies*, 8:1 (2000), pp. 29-42.

Vertigans, S. and Sutton, P. W., 'Globalisation Theory and Islamic Praxis', *Global Society*, 16:1 (2002), pp. 31-46.

Viesti, G., 'Economic Policies and Local Development: Some Reflections', *European Planning Studies*, 10:4 (2002), pp. 467-481.

Vines, S., *The Years of Living Dangerously: Asia - From Financial Crisis to the New Millennium*, London, Orion Business, 1999.

Warschauer, M., 'Singapore's Dilemma: Control versus Autonomy in IT-Led Development', *The Information Society*, 17:4 (2001), pp. 305-311.

Werbner, P., 'What Colour "Success"? Distorting Value in Studies of Ethnic Entrepreneurship', *The Sociological Review*, 47:3 (1999), pp. 548-579.

World Bank, 'World Development Indicators: Science and Technology', (2001), http://www.worldbank.org/data/wdi2001/index.htm

World Bank, 'World Development Indicators: The Information Age', (2000), http://www.worldbank.org/data/wdi2000/statesmkts.htm

Yao, X., 'Who is a Confucian Today? A Critical Reflection on the Issues Concerning Confucian Identity in Modern Times', *Journal of Contemporary Religion*, 16:3 (2001), pp. 313-328.

Yeoh, B. S. A. and Chang, T. C., 'Globalising Singapore: Debating Transnational Flows in the City', *Urban Studies*, 38:7 (2001), pp. 1025-1044.

Yeung, H. W-C., 'The Dynamics of Asian Business Systems in a Globalizing Era', *Review of International Political Economy*, 7:3 (2000a), pp. 399-433.

Yeung, H. W-C., 'Embedding Foreign Affiliates in Transnational Business Networks: the Case of Hong Kong Firms in Southeast Asia', *Environment and Planning A*, 32:2 (2000b), pp. 201-222.

Yeung, H. W-C., 'Transnational Economic Synergy and Business Networks: The Case of Two-way Investment Between Malaysia and Singapore', *Regional Studies*, 32:8 (1998), pp. 687-706.

Yeung, H. W-C., Poon, J. and Perry, M., 'Towards a Regional Strategy: The Role of Regional Headquarters of Foreign Firms in Singapore', *Urban Studies*, 38:1 (2001), pp. 157-183.

Yeung, M. T., Perdikis, N. and Kerr, W. A., *Regional Trading Blocs in the Global Economy of the EU and ASEAN*, Cheltenham, Edward Elgar, 1999.

Appendix

Factor Analyses

Table A.1.1: Factor Analysis of the West of England Data Survey
   Principal Component Factor Analysis Sorted Rotated Factor Loadings

Variables	*Factor 1*	*Factor 2*	*Factor 3*
INN	*0.805*	-0.138	0.007
REGR&DPT	*0.758*	0.085	0.007
LEMPL	*0.722*	0.166	-0.312
BRINN	*0.614*	-0.211	-0.376
COLSUP	-0.048	*0.866*	0.066
SKILSTAR	0.298	*0.709*	0.277
SKILLED	0.295	*-0.671*	0.360
REGCAFE	0.115	0.130	*-0.828*
EMBED	0.169	-0.229	*-0.773*
Explained			
Variability (%)	**26%**	**21%**	**19%**

Source: Statistical processing of own survey.
Note: Values represent the factor loading of each variable on each of the factors. Factors with large coefficients (in absolute values) are shown in bold italics and are closely related to their corresponding variables.

Table A.1.2: Cluster Analyses of the West of England Data Survey

A (with principal factors derived from the factor analysis)

	Number of observations	Within cluster sum of squares	Average distance from centroid
Cluster 1	23	37.074	1.206
Cluster 2	23	41.351	1.239
Cluster 3	15	22.157	1.133
Centroids			
Variable	**Cluster 1**	**Cluster 2**	**Cluster 3**
INNOCO	-0.3660	-0.3629	1.1177
SUPCHACO	**0.9664**	-0.6522	-0.4818
ISOLCO	-0.2418	**0.6970**	-0. 6979

B *(with original variables)*

	Number of observations	Within cluster sum of squares	Average distance from centroid
Cluster 1	23	128.885	2.299
Cluster 2	24	141.800	2.383
Cluster 3	14	85.460	2.397

Centroids Variable	Cluster 1	Cluster 2	Cluster 3
INN	-0.2959	-0.3146	*1.0254*
REGR&DPT	0.1250	*-0.5179*	*0.6824*
COLSUP	*1.1129*	*-0.7174*	*-0.5986*
SKILSTAR	*-0.4731*	*-0.5306*	-0.1146
REGCAFE	0.0376	-0.4087	*0.6388*
EMBED	-0.3788	-0.0824	*0.7636*
LEMPL	0.1209	*-0.6275*	*0.8770*
BRINN	-0.4392	-0.4392	*1.4743*

Source: Statistical processing of own survey.
Note: Values in the lower part of tables represent the average value of each variable for each group of firms. Large coefficients are shown in bold italics.

Table A.1.3: Factor Analysis of the Singapore-Johor Data Survey
Principal Component Factor Analysis Sorted Rotated Factor Loadings

Variables	*Factor 1*	*Factor 2*	*Factor 3*
OWNRQ	*0.777*	-0.370	0.029
NEWPR	*0.755*	0.195	0.451
OWNMQ	*0.728*	-0.322	-0.222
RAVSTF	*0.703*	0.449	-0.503
SKILL	*0.664*	0.553	0.282
OWNMME	*0.623*	-0.604	-0.195
RQUSTF	*0.609*	0.448	-0.577
RSETUP	-0.548	*0.672*	-0.205
RDI	0.516	0.317	*0.633*
Explained Variability (%)	**44%**	**21%**	**16%**

Source: Statistical processing of own survey.
Note: Values represent the factor loading of each variable on each of the factors. Factors with large coefficients (in absolute values) are shown in bold italics and are closely related to their corresponding variables.

Table A.1.4: Cluster Analyses of the Singapore-Johor Data Survey

A (with principal factors derived from the factor analysis)

	Number of observations	Within cluster sum of squares	Average distance from centroid
Cluster 1	11	9.948	0.849
Cluster 2	7	6.153	0.901
Cluster 3	12	28.586	1.381

Centroids Variable	**Cluster 1**	**Cluster 2**	**Cluster 3**
LOCSTART	0.1384	**0.8471**	-0.6210
SETUPCO	0.6533	-1.1872	**0.0937**
INDINNO	**0.9427**	-0.0850	-0.8145

B (with original variables)

	Number of observations	Within cluster sum of squares	Average distance from centroid
Cluster 1	12	36.123	1.585
Cluster 2	8	33.606	2.032
Cluster 3	10	63.800	63.800

Centroids Variable	**Cluster 1**	**Cluster 2**	**Cluster 3**
SKILL	-0.1629	-0.5836	**0.6624**
NEWPR	-0.4825	-0.2836	**0.8059**
RDI	-0.3072	-0.3007	**0.6092**
RAVSTF	-0.1226	-1.0418	**0.9805**
RQUSTF	-0.1226	-1.1587	**0.8365**
OWNRQ	-0.9197	0.0657	1.0511
OWNMME	-0.7555	**0.3120**	0.6569
RSETUP	**0.9891**	-0.6594	-0.6594
OWNMQ	-0.6952	-0.1738	**0.9733**

Source: Statistical processing of own survey.

Note: Values in the lower part of tables represent the average value of each variable for each group of firms. Large coefficients are shown in bold italics.

Index

A

Aalborg group, 15
agglomeration economies, 1, 14, 15, 106
American multinationals, 95
APEC, 6, 48
ASEAN, 1, 2, 3, 5, 6, 7, 20, 23, 24, 25, 34, 35, 36, 38, 42, 44, 46, 47, 48, 49, 50, 54, 97, 101, 103, 105, 110, 112, 114, 115
Asian values, 104, 109
Asia-Pacific region, 36, 39
associationalism, 103
Aztech, 8

B

Baden-Württemberg, 1, 14
BAe, 7, 32
Bank Negara Malaysia, 40
Bath, 21, 50, 53, 54, 56, 63, 96
behaviour, 3, 4, 5, 10, 13, 16, 18, 20, 25, 28, 45, 85, 86, 87, 88, 90, 91, 94, 95, 98, 99, 101, 102, 110, 113, 114
Bintan and Batam, 24, 42
breakthrough innovations, 4, 53, 55, 56, 71, 89, 97, 114
Bristol, 21, 24, 33, 48, 50, 51, 53, 54, 55, 96
Bumiputra, 38
business networks, 19, 20, 45
Butchard, 54

C

cafeteria effect, 10, 61, 80
California, 13, 17, 24
Calori, 103
Cambridge, 1, 13, 18, 24, 97
Capello, 4, 5, 9, 10, 11
Caraça, 26
Catalonia, 14, 19
Cheltenham, 24, 33, 53, 55, 95

Chinese business networks, 19
cluster analysis, 87, 89, 90, 91, 93, 94, 112
cluster policies, 14, 33
clusters, 1, 3, 4, 13, 14, 15, 24, 35, 36, 37, 60, 62, 69, 89, 91, 93, 97
collaborative learning, 3, 4, 53, 104
collective learning, 3, 4, 5, 8, 9, 10, 11, 13, 16, 17, 18, 53, 59, 63, 69, 73, 81, 82, 85, 89, 90, 91, 94, 97, 98, 99, 106
Compaq, 8
complementarities, 44, 45, 94, 103
Confucian values, 109, 115
Creative Technology, 8
Cyprus, 13

D

Da Cunha, 44
Dosi, 11
Dublin, 24
Dupont Electronics, 32
Dupuy and Gilly, 16
Dyson, 7, 17, 33, 55

E

Economic Development Board, 37, 39, 40, 82, 118
embeddedness, 10, 24, 88, 91, 106
Emilia-Romagna, 23
EMU, 1, 9, 27, 111
entrepreneurs, 5, 9, 15, 17, 82, 84, 85, 100, 114
entrepreneurship, 1, 7, 8, 31, 65, 85, 95, 114, 115
EU, 1, 2, 3, 6, 14, 23, 24, 25, 27, 28, 29, 30, 31, 32, 34, 46, 47, 48, 49, 103, 107, 110, 111, 113
EU-ASEAN, 1, 2, 5, 23, 25, 46, 47
European Commission, 3, 29, 47, 49, 107, 110
European regional policy, 29
European Union, 1, 3, 27, 28, 30, 34, 47, 48, 49, 107, 112. See EU
evolutionary school, 5, 12

F

factor analysis, 87, 88, 89, 91, 92
FDI, 42, 48
Feser, 13
Fordist, 10, 12
Foreign Direct Investment (FDI), 2, 38, 41, 42, 47, 48, 105. See FDI
Friedmann, 16

G

General System of Preferences, 48
geographical proximity, 9, 10, 13, 16, 18, 24, 29, 42, 43, 44, 85, 98
globalisation, 1, 2, 14, 23, 27, 28, 36, 97, 98, 101, 104, 106, 107, 108, 110, 113, 114, 115
GNK-Westland, 7, 32
Goh Chock Tong, 109
Grabher and Stark, 16, 19
Granovetter, 19
GREMI, 8, 9, 11, 16, 18, 82
Grunsven, 41, 42, 43

H

Haley and Low, 108, 109
Hamilton-Hart, 109
Hewlett Packard, 7, 8, 32
high-technology SMEs, 2, 4, 5, 17, 53, 65, 71, 74, 82, 83, 85, 87, 90, 91, 98, 99, 102, 104, 113, 114
Hofstede, 103
Honda, 7, 32

I

IBM, 8, 79
industrial district, 1, 9, 10, 13, 14, 21, 24, 31, 69, 87, 95
innovation
breakthrough, 4, 9, 17, 53, 54, 56, 71, 72, 89, 90, 97, 114
incremental, 9, 12, 17
linear model of innovation, 26
national systems of innovation, 15, 26
radical, 13, 17
innovative milieu, 2, 4, 5, 8, 9, 10, 11, 12,

13, 15, 16, 18, 23, 24, 42, 53, 54, 58, 61, 64, 69, 70, 73, 79, 82, 67, 89, 91, 94, 95, 96, 97, 99, 101, 104, 113
innovative performance, 3, 32, 49, 50, 55, 71, 110
Intel, 7, 27, 32

J

Japanese multinationals, 26
Johanson, 12
Johor, 1, 2, 3, 4, 5, 8, 14, 20, 24, 25, 41, 42, 43, 44, 45, 46, 50, 53, 69, 70, 71, 72, 73, 74, 78, 79, 80, 81, 82, 83, 85, 87, 91, 92, 93, 94, 95, 97, 98, 99, 100, 101, 102, 103, 104, 105, 110, 111, 112, 113
Johor Bahru, 42, 44, 69, 70, 71, 72, 73, 80, 97
Johor Strait, 44

K

Kamann, 10, 11, 12
Kanter, 15, 16, 19, 99
Keppel Corporation, 43
Knoke, 19
knowledge-based economy, 1, 3, 4, 5, 20, 23, 24, 25, 33, 34, 37, 38, 49, 63, 98, 101, 103, 105, 107, 108, 110, 113, 114
Kuala Lumpur, 14, 46, 50
Kukli_ski, 24, 106, 107, 108

L

labour mobility, 10, 18, 43, 64
Lagendijk, 14
Lawson, 8, 11, 18, 33
learning
learning-by-doing, 12
learning-by-interacting, 12
learning-by-using, 12
learning for innovation, 23, 24, 86, 109
Lee Kuan Yew, 44, 108, 109
linear model of innovation - see Innovation
linkages, 1, 2, 8, 10, 16, 18, 19, 39, 42, 43, 53, 66, 69, 74, 79, 80, 84, 99, 113
links, 2, 10, 11, 15, 29, 40, 42, 43, 46, 48, 61, 62, 64, 66, 78, 79, 80, 84, 85, 99, 104

Linotype-Hell, 55
Ljungkvist, 48
Logica, 32
Lombardy, 19
Lucent Technologies, 7, 32
Lundvall, 15, 16
Lundvall and Johnson, 16

M
M4/M5 corridors, 2, 3
Mahathir, 40, 109, 110, 114
Malaysia's Vision 2020, 40
Malecki, 19, 61
market culture, 5, 25, 33, 102, 103, 104, 105, 114
Marshall, 8, 9
Matsushita, 8
Meeus, 49, 59
Messier-Dowty, 7, 32
metropolitan agglomerations, 11
milieux, 4, 5, 8, 9, 10, 11, 12, 13, 16, 17, 18, 24, 79, 80, 87, 89, 95, 99, 101, 104, 112
Mining Corporation, 43
Morgan, 16
Motorola, 7, 8, 32
Multimedia Super Corridor, 14, 40

N
national systems of innovation - see Innovation
NEC, 8
Nelson and Winter, 11
networks, 10, 11, 12, 14, 15, 18, 19, 20, 21, 28, 29, 30, 32, 40, 45, 46, 59, 61, 62, 63, 66, 74, 80, 85, 86, 98, 99, 102, 103, 104, 107, 113, 114, 115
New Economic Policy, 38, 105

O
Oxford, 1, 18, 24, 95

P
Philips, 8, 36, 79
Port of Singapore Authority, 112

Porter, 13, 14, 15, 37
Post-Fordist, 10
Putnam, 16, 19

R
R&D, 1, 13, 14, 23, 25, 26, 31, 32, 35, 37, 38, 39, 45, 48, 50, 55, 56, 57, 61, 66, 67, 71, 72, 73, 85, 89, 92, 94, 97, 98, 99, 104, 105, 113
R&D department, 13, 31, 55, 57, 61, 66, 71, 72, 73, 85, 89
Rabellotti, 4, 8, 9
Racal, 7, 55, 95
Racal-Thorn, 7
Raychem, 55
Regional Development Agency, 32, 33, 37, 50, 104
regional integration, 1, 6, 44, 103
regional specialisation, 14, 103
regionalisation, 26, 28, 30, 37, 41, 42, 43, 105, 113
regression analysis, 87
Renishaw, 7, 33, 95
research and development - see R&D
Riau, 1, 2, 24, 41, 42, 43, 105
Rolls Royce, 7, 32
Rotork, 7

S
Schumpeter, 8, 12
Seagate, 8
Sengenberger and Pyke, 12
Siemens, 8
SIJORI triangle, 24, 42, 43, 69, 97
Silicon Fen, 13
Silicon Valley, 1, 12, 13, 14, 17, 21, 24, 106
Sime Darby Bhd, 43
Singapore Airlines, 112
Singapore Technology Group, 43
Singapore-Johor, 1, 2, 3, 4, 5, 8, 20, 25, 42, 43, 44, 45, 46, 53, 69, 70, 71, 73,74, 78, 79, 80, 82, 83, 84, 85, 87, 91, 92, 93, 94, 96, 97, 98, 99, 100, 101, 102, 103, 104, 105, 110, 112, 113
Singapore-Johor-Riau growth triangle, 1, 2
SingTel, 8

Smiths Industries, 7, 95
Sony, 8
Sophia-Antipolis, 1
South-East Asia, 1, 2, 5, 7, 14, 19, 24, 36, 37, 41, 42, 44, 46, 48, 49, 50, 69, 86, 101, 102, 105, 106, 108, 109, 110, 113
South Wales, 1, 2, 5, 24, 56
South West of England, 1, 3, 5, 7, 14, 15, 21, 24, 31, 32, 34, 37, 49, 53, 54, 55, 56, 62, 98, 103, 104
Steiner, 14
STMicroelectronics, 7, 8
Storper, 11, 15, 21
Streeck and Schmitter, 19
sub-regional agglomeration, 3, 96
Swindon, 21, 24, 33, 50, 53, 54, 55, 96

T

technological change, 8, 11, 12, 15, 109 34
technological development, 10, 12, 15, 38, 39, 40, 102, 105, 108, 110
technological innovation, 8, 9, 23, 25, 26, 27, 29, 64
technological knowledge, 24, 36
technological policies, 5, 20, 23, 30, 101, 103
Technological policy, 4, 14, 16, 25, 27, 34
Third Italy, 1
Third World, 36
Thorn-EMI, 55
Thurow, 25, 107, 108, 109, 111
TNCs, 2, 32, 35, 36, 38, 40, 41, 42, 43, 44, 45, 46, 50, 69, 75, 79, 86, 94, 97, 98, 102, 105, 112, 114
transnational co-operation, 29
transnational corporations (TNCs) - see TNCs

U

UK, 5, 18, 14, 26, 27, 31, 32, 38, 47, 48, 67, 95, 98. See United Kingdom
UMNO, 109, 114
UMW Corporation, 43
United States, 36, 39, 46, 85, 107, 110
United Kingdom, 6, 24. See UK.

W

Washington Post, 29
West of England, 1, 2, 3, 4, 5, 7, 8, 15, 19, 20, 21, 24, 25, 31, 32, 34, 37, 48, 49, 53, 54, 55, 56, 57, 58, 59, 61, 62, 63, 64, 65, 66, 70, 71, 72, 73, 74, 75, 80, 84, 85, 86, 87, 88, 90, 91, 95, 96, 97, 98, 99, 100, 101, 102, 103, 104, 110, 113, 115

Y

Yeung, 19, 29, 34, 35, 43, 47, 48, 86, 110